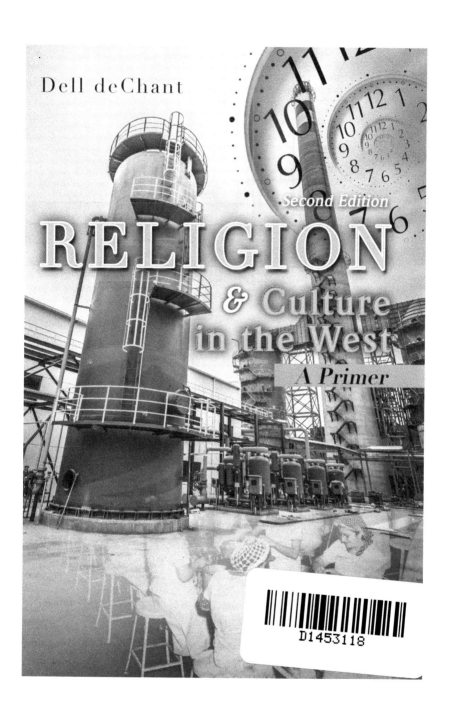

Dell deChant

Second Edition

RELIGION
& Culture in the West
in the West

A Primer

Kendall Hunt
publishing company

To all my students

And was Jerusalem builded here
Among these dark Satanic mills?
                    —William Blake, from "Jerusalem"

Contents

Foreword

Religion, enigmatically from a scholarly standpoint, remains exceptionally viable and tremendously influential in the world today—even in the modernized and secularized West. No adequate scholarly understanding of world affairs, culture, society, particular institutions, or the individual can afford to ignore the role and significance of religion. Scholarly debates about religion, its place in culture and society, and closely related matters are central to social theorizing about the radical transformation of human affairs that produced modern societies. Those classic discussions and disagreements about them continue today in even greater complexity as contemporary thinkers seek to describe, interpret, and understand the present and the future of human existence and especially the role of religion in it all.

In this brief work, Dell deChant demonstrates mastery of the more central and salient issues presented in these multifaceted and sometimes dense scholarly discussions of religion and culture in the Western world today. Reflecting an unusual gift for sharing this knowledge with others he concisely and cogently outlines and illuminates what is at stake in these matters. The presentation is unpretentious, and it makes these complex issues highly accessible, even to the uninitiated, without being overly simplistic. This account of culture and religion in the West is balanced, reflecting different and often times emotionally charged oppositional viewpoints. DeChant, however, does not become embroiled in the associated polemics, and he does not seek to resolve the differences. He thereby invites the readers to carefully consider different theoretical perspectives and viewpoints, become engaged in these important scholarly issues, formulate their own positions, and draw their own conclusions.

Yet, this work is much more than merely a concise and well-organized summary of the bigger issues and better scholarship on culture and religion in the West. It genuinely reflects a creative approach to these complex matters resulting in truly novel meanings and interpretations. Although it will be of tremendous value to upper-division undergraduate and beginning graduate students, advanced graduate students and other teaching and research scholars also will find it useful and even stimulating; I did. After digesting deChant's innovative presentation of these issues, I promptly revised several of my undergraduate and graduate courses, based on new insights, with positive and profitable results. Likewise, my thinking about several research problems of long-standing interest has changed and benefited from this brief but timely piece of scholarship. Other readers from diverse educational backgrounds and disciplines, no doubt, will find deChant's scholarship of tremendous merit, too.

Danny L. Jorgensen, Ph.D.
Professor of Religious Studies
University of South Florida

Preface

The second edition of *Religion and Culture in the West: A Primer* follows the first by seven years. The world has changed considerably in this time, and the importance of understanding the relationship of religion and culture in the West is of even more critical importance now than it was seven years ago.

As a primer, this book offers an introduction to this relationship, and a review of some of the ways this relationship may be understood. It is a survey, an outline, and an overview. It presents a wide variety of approaches to the topic and differing interpretations. I have endeavored to keep my own interpretations out of the text, although to a certain extent that is unavoidable. As explained more fully in the introduction, one of the goals of the book is to include material often missing from introductory texts on this subject, while also covering traditional topics. Besides that, my hope is that this primer will serve as something of a welcome to the study of religion and culture in the West, and more generally, the study of religion.

Thirty years ago, I became convinced that in order to understand the world and reflect on its future, the study of religion was an absolute necessity. Today, I am even more convinced of the importance of studying religion. There is nothing we more urgently need to understand than religion. The second edition of this little book aims to contribute to this understanding.

Religion & Culture in the West: A Primer would not exist were it not for the assistance of others. It would neither have been started nor completed without the inspiration, encouragement, and support of a number of people. Who to thank first and how to arrange the sequence of acknowledgements is always difficult for me. Everyone included here has been helpful, and no ranking is implied by the arrangement.

In the most general sense, I am indebted to Professor Darrell J. Fasching—not only for this book but also for many of my other publications in this general area. It was Dr. Fasching who first stimulated my interest in the study of religion and culture over a quarter of a century ago, and he has never ceased to take an active interest in my research. He has always been willing to review my work, and was among the first to review the manuscript of this book. As always, his critiques and suggestions for improvement were invaluable. Thankfully, Darrell and I do not always see things quite the same way, which makes his reading of my work all the more helpful.

Another longtime colleague, Professor Danny L. Jorgensen, was particularly helpful to the completion of this book. It was Dr. Jorgensen who initially suggested that I consider putting together something along the lines of this primer. As the book began to take shape, his encouragement was unfailing. At the practical level, Danny brought to my attention several texts that proved to be extremely beneficial to the development of several sections of the book. Like Darrell, Danny was one of the first to evaluate and critique the manuscript. Danny and I also have our disagreements, and they are different from the ones I have with Darrell; and different again from the ones that Danny and Darrell have with each other. What could be merrier! The end result, however, is that this book is better for having critical evaluations from them both.

The book benefited from a third critical reading. This one was by one of my former graduate students, Mr. Don Surrency. As I was beginning work in earnest on the book, Don was putting the finishing touches on his MA thesis, "The Proliferating Sacred: Secularization and Postmodernity." As will be evident when reading this book (especially the latter parts), Don was uniquely prepared to evaluate my manuscript. In fact, it is fair to say that my work with Don on his thesis was a major motivation to the completion of my book. Don's critique was especially insightful—and meaningful.

Another former graduate student, Ms. Michelle Demeter, not only offered insightful criticisms, but also voluntarily copyedited the entire manuscript in a remarkably short period of time. Michelle and I have worked together on numerous projects over the years and she has never failed to speed those projects to completion with both vigor and grace. Finally, this second edition was improved by new material on several topics. Of special note are additions to the analysis of the secularization dispute, in chapter four. Here, I am indebted to another former student, and now PhD candidate, Mr. Nicholas Bile, for helping me understand and articulate nuances in the dispute.

Earlier versions of several sections of the book were published in *The Sacred Santa,* originally by The Pilgrim Press (2002) and later by Wipf and Stock Publishers (2008). I am appreciative of The Pilgrim Press, and especially its publisher, Timothy Staveteig, for the release of the production rights of the book, allowing for the inclusion of these sections.

Special thanks are extended to Kendall/Hunt Publishing Company. I appreciate Kendall/Hunt's early and ongoing commitment to this book. Everyone associated with Kendall/Hunt has been most helpful, from the initial contacts, through the editing and final revisions, including the outstanding design for the cover.

I also must thank all my students—those who have studied with me over the past 29 years, those who study with me now, and those who will study with me in the future. Their desire to learn about religion and seek out its meaning never ceases to thrill and motivate me. They are a source of perpetual inspiration. This book is dedicated to them.

Finally, I thank my wife and partner in life, Marilynn. From first to last, she assisted me in tangible and intangible ways. She talked with me about the incipient idea of the book, listened to me read parts aloud, reviewed the earliest drafts, put up with my working late for too many nights (and just generally put up with my overfull schedule), reviewed the cover art, and finally, proofread the final draft of the manuscript. All this, while running her own business and serving on our city council. I cannot thank her enough. The book would not have happened without her.

Introduction

As the title indicates, this book is a primer on religion and culture in the West. In this regard, it is reasonable to say just a bit about what its status as a primer means. First, here is what it is not. It is not intended to be an exhaustive or detailed study of the subject. This is not a work of theory, although a number of theories will be presented. It is also not a product of original research, although it will survey a fair amount of research done by others. This book is not in that ball game (to use a sports metaphor) when it comes to the study of religion and culture, and does not aspire to be so. It is in the ball park where the game is played, however, and it aspires to tell readers a little bit about this game and to do so in an original manner.

I have played the game myself, and continue to, but I have spent much more time in the stands as an engaged and knowledgeable spectator—a fan, if you will. I know how the game is played, the teams, the players, the rules, and a fair amount of its history. The intent of this book is to present the most elementary features of this game to readers who are less familiar with it than I. I can also confess, and to bring this metaphorical adventure with sports to a close, I love this game.

Readers will quickly discover that topics dealt with here are not without controversy. In several areas there is disagreement, and in some instances, considerable debate. The controversial issues and points of disagreement have not been ignored or glossed over. They are, after all, part of the terrain and necessary features of this area of inquiry. In dealing with differing positions, I have endeavored to remain neutral and present each stance fairly and accurately. Where there is conflict, every effort has been made to represent all sides of an issue to their best advantage, including selections from representative texts by the thinkers involved. I do not believe that this approach has led to a misrepresentation of the significance (or in some cases the intensity) of the disagreements. They are very real and very important, and they do make a difference in how the study of this subject has developed and where it may be headed. Finally, although I certainly have my own views on these issues and evaluate some positions as superior to others, I have refrained from advancing my own interpretations or developing arguments for or against the positions presented here. Readers who desire to further explore points of disagreement and controversy presented here are directed to the primary sources cited in the text. For those interested in my own position on various issues presented here, access to my work should not be too difficult.

Turning now to what this text is, or at least what it intends to be, the most important initial observation, again, is found in the part of the title after the colon. This is a primer. Readers are not expected to have any prior familiarity with the subject or academic texts dealing with culture or religion. You do not need to be a specialist to read and understand this book. As a primer, *Religion & Culture in the West: A Primer* is designed to serve as a short, basic introduction to and overview of the academic study of the relationship between religion and Western (Euro-American) culture. Basic technical terms are defined, major theories are explicated, and central issues are highlighted. Throughout the book, works by selected thinkers are referenced and excerpts presented. Hopefully, readers will delve further into these works as a result of reading this primer. Ideally, some will even study the theories and engage the issues introduced here.

Although scholarly topics and theoretical issues are central to this text, I have tried to present them using a style and language accessible to general readers. In this regard, this is a book for anyone with an interest in this area but little or no prior knowledge. Most readers will probably encounter it in classroom settings, as a textbook in courses on religion. Its professional audience will include clerics and other religious professionals, government officials and civil servants, media professionals, and possibly persons in financial services. Scholars in the humanities and social sciences may find it helpful as a refresher text, and those in other fields may find it useful as a source for general understandings of the cultural context of their research. Still, most persons picking up this book will be students in undergraduate college courses in such areas as religious studies, humanities, theology, and also possibly sociology, history, and political science.

Aside from serving as a general introductory text, *Religion & Culture in the West: A Primer* also aims to fill several small but distinct gaps in literature on this subject. In order to do this, the text presents relatively well-established scholarly understandings using an arrangement and presentation strategy that is original in several ways. In pursuit of this aim, the text is divided into four chapters and a coda.

The first chapter offers a summary of generally accepted understandings of the relationship between culture, society, and religion, giving special attention to the various approaches that have been used to define and analyze religion. In itself, this approach is somewhat uncommon, but what makes it particularly distinctive is its inclusion of a fairly detailed explication of the contrasts between cosmological and transcendental religions as both historical phenomena and theoretic categories. These contrasts are explored further in Chapter 2 in the context of one of the great turning points in history, the Axial Age. This period is cited in a number of primary texts, but it seldom is presented in as much detail as it will be here. An exposition of the secularization thesis is offered in Chapter 3. The exposition follows the standard account of the thesis, so there is nothing particularly novel there, although certain details and emphases in this primer are not found in other versions of the standard account. Review of the debate about the contemporary viability of the secularization thesis, presented in Chapter 4, is rather unique, largely for its neutral framing of positions in the debate and also because the review does not serve as a preface to a new position brought forward in continuity or contrast with others. Finally, beginning in Chapter 4 and continuing through the Coda, I have contextualized the status of religion and culture in the contemporary West in terms of postmodern theory, *religious resurgence,* and neo-cosmological concepts of the sacred, bringing together several lines of inquiry that usually are quite independent of each other. Following the text, in Appendix I, is Leonard Swidler's "Dialogue Decalogue," which offers invaluable guidelines to the study of religion in a pluralistic culture. Appendix II contains a series of question-helps for students, and general readers.

I do not expect this primer to resolve any of the issues it surveys. It is not designed to do that. It is designed to familiarize readers with these issues, and perhaps to inspire some to engage them on their own.

1
Understanding Religion in a Cultural Context

Culture, Society, and Religion

Understanding the relationship of religion and culture appropriately begins with consideration of the terms themselves. Although the term *religion* appears first in the title of this primer, and it may seem reasonable to define it prior to *culture,* for this study, it will be more helpful to first consider culture, then (in more detail) religion. The conception of culture put forward here is hardly the only one available, although it is consistent with others advanced in various texts that consider the relationship between religion and culture. Of particular note are treatments by Peter Berger, Bruce David Forbes, and H. Richard Niebuhr,[1] although definitions given in a number of other sources (including the standard, *Webster's New Collegiate Dictionary*[2]) are not appreciably different. Readers are invited to peruse these sources for more detailed studies of the concept of culture.

In continuity with these sources, culture is here understood as *the human-made world.* More specifically, culture is the collective entirety of human products, both material and non-material. Everything made by human beings is included under this heading; from Robert Zund's *The Road to Emmaus* to Kanye West's "Jesus Walks"; from Adam Smith's economic theories to the subprime mortgage crisis; from language to cellphones; from hoes to assembly lines; and from

1

William Blake's "dark Satanic mills" to the New York City skyline. Importantly, this concept of culture recognizes that it is collective, and includes both concrete material products as well as elements in human consciousness. Culture, then, is objective, subjective, and intersubjective; it is material and mental, concrete and symbolic.

In addition to this brief explication, there are three other basic features of culture of critical importance to the study of religion and culture presented here. First, culture is not a collection of discrete elements but, rather, a comprehensive whole that articulates the dimensions and details of individual and collective existence. It includes the material objects we possess or long for, the dreams we have, the music to which we listen, the beliefs we accept, and so on; but it is also the overall symbolic framework in which these diverse elements are ordered and patterned in an intelligible and meaningful manner. As a related note in this regard, *culture* can be used both generally (human culture) or in reference to specific communities defined in a variety of ways and with varying degrees of precision (e.g., Chinese culture, medieval culture, Islamic culture, early twentieth-century American urban culture).

Second, society is a human product—an element of culture. As a human creation, society is a part of culture, albeit a most critical (perhaps the *most* critical) one. As Berger succinctly notes: "Man cannot exist apart from society."[3] Society is the cultural feature that structures human activity, allowing human beings to create, organize, and control their world by way of collectives and groups. Society supplies the guidelines through which persons live and work together in harmony, and through which they educate (literally, *socialize*) children about facts and values of community life, thus transmitting those facts and values to the next generation. Through society, the overall symbolic framework of culture (noted above) is articulated and maintained and, through *socialization,* this framework is projected into the future. There is, thus, a synergistic relationship between culture and society. Society is a part of culture, and culture depends on society for its maintenance and continuation.

Third, as a phenomenon within society, and like society as a whole, religion is a human product, and properly classified as an element of culture. Since the rest of this chapter will be devoted to various conceptions of religion, and these will serve to locate religion in a cultural context, the relationship between religion, culture, and society will be considered only briefly at this point. This being said, the traditional relationship between religion and society is not unlike the relationship between society and culture. In other words, as society is a critical element of culture, religion is a critical element of society, serving as part of its ongoing enterprise of organizing human activity. It has also traditionally been a critical feature of culture, per se, serving as the source of ideas, beliefs, and myths that are intrinsic to the overall symbolic framework of culture. In this way, for the vast bulk of human existence, religion has served as the primary source of foundational support for human culture and society. Sociologists refer to this sort of support as *legitimation,* by which they mean the process through which cultural understandings and social arrangements (large or small, oppressive or liberating, passive or assertive) are justified, especially in instances when they are questioned.

Historically, religion has supplied human culture with the ultimate sort of legitimation by locating cultural systems and their social structures in the context of a sacred (ultimate) order of existence. As Clifford Geertz explains the process (using "cosmic" rather than "sacred"), "religion tunes human actions to an envisaged cosmic order and projects images of cosmic order onto the plane of human experience."[4] This can be called *sacred legitimation.* Most bluntly, sacred legitimation states that things are the way they are because of the order of creation itself as established by the ultimate power.

When questioned, the range of answers given to legitimate cultural systems and their social structures are too numerous to mention. Here are a few more common ones (you can supply the appropriate question): It is the way the universe was set up, it is against human nature, it is God's will, it is the outworking of karma, it is a violation of the sacred code, it is the way the ancestors did it, and so on. Behind every question of order and propriety and every regressive sequence of such questions is a final answer that rules out all subsequent questions and ends all questioning: It is the way the ultimate power arranged the universe and with it the human world as well. As explained by my co-author (Darrell Fasching) in *Comparative Religious Ethics: A Narrative Approach,* "the sacred sacralizes the finite order of society, seeing a society's way of life as an expression of the sacred cosmic order of things. And what is sacred is held to be beyond question."[5]

In summary, then, culture is the collective entirety of human products, including both material and nonmaterial products, that articulates the dimensions and the details of our existence. Society is a component part of culture, and it is of extreme importance because it supplies the framework by which human life and culture is structured, maintained, and projected into the future. Historically, religion has served as the primary source of support for human societies through its capacity to supply a sacred legitimation for the social order. On the basis of these working understandings, religion can now be considered in more detail.

Three Approaches to Defining Religion

It is not uncommon in books on religion to find passages to the effect that religion is difficult to define or there are so many definitions of religion that it is challenging to come up with a single one that is satisfactory. Those books make a good point. The concept of religion is notoriously ambiguous, there are numerous definitions, and it is difficult to isolate one that is entirely satisfactory. The very word, *religion*, is culturally relative, and, as will be considered later, the existence of religion as an independent institution is a relatively rare and recent occurrence over the great sweep of human history. Nonetheless, the specification of a working understanding of religion is necessary in a study of this type.

Before considering various definitions and descriptions of religion and offering one for purposes of this inquiry, it will be helpful to consider three general types of definition—functional, substantive, and formal. As defined by Steve Bruce: "Functional definitions identify religion in terms of what it does," and "[s]ubstantive definitions identify religion in terms of what it is."[6] Bruce analyzes both types and explains that each has challenges. As he correctly observes, in a general sense, functional definitions tend to be too broad and substantive definitions tend to be too culturally limited.[7] Daniel L. Pals also offers a helpful sketch of these two types of definitions, which is in general agreement with Bruce, noting that functional definitions are concerned with how religion "operates in human life," while substantive definitions focus on "the beliefs and ideas that religious people commit to and find important."[8] Catherine Albanese's explication of the types of definitions includes functional and substantive (in general agreement with Bruce and Pals) and adds the third type, formal. Her explication is particularly valuable in the detail it gives on each of the types, its inclusion of the formal type, and the specification of the specialists who tend to favor each type. As she explains:

> Substantive definitions of religion focus on the inner core, essence, or nature of religion and define it by this thing-in-itself. They tend to emphasize a relationship with a higher being or beings (God or the Gods) and to be favored by theologians and philosophers. Functional definitions of religions emphasize the effects of religion in actual life. They stress the systems of meaning-making that religion provides and how it helps people deal with the ills, insecurities, and catastrophes of living. Functional definitions of religion are favored by scholars in the social sciences. Lastly, formal definitions of religion look for typically religious forms gleaned from the comparative

study of religions and find the presence of religion where such forms can be identified. Religious forms include sacred stories, rituals, moral codes, and communities; and formal definitions of religion tend to be favored by historians of religion.[9]

Definitions of Religion: A Sampling

Turning now to how religion is actually defined, it is helpful to bear in mind the initial challenge, which was mentioned earlier: Religion is difficult to define, and there is a multitude of different definitions.[10] There is no single standard definition of religion. A sampling of definitions will be presented here, followed by a provisional description.

The definitions considered here are all good, workable definitions, and each has merits and deficiencies. All have been offered by notable scholars of religion and many of these definitions have been adopted by others. Many have been critiqued, some extensively. The intent of this text is not to critique or offer an in-depth analysis of the definitions. Instead, it aims simply to present the definitions and unpack them a bit to expose readers to some of the classic understandings of religion, as well as others that will help illuminate the variety of ways in which religion has been academically defined. The survey will also supply a context for the provisional description of religion that subsequently will be used in the book.

The first definitions are those appropriately classified as *classic*. These have been advanced by thinkers who have had a significant influence on the academic study of religion. Several are quite well known, even outside the circle of religious scholars. Readers will find these definitions frequently cited (or referred to) in texts dealing with definitions of religion, and it is not uncommon to find some introduced as the understanding of religion that a particular scholar will use in a specific study. Besides those covered here, there are many others that qualify as classics. These are but a sample, and aside from their general value to the development of the academic study of religion, it is worth noting that they have been of particular influence on the provisional description of religion, which will be presented at the close of this chapter.

One of the most well-known figures in the intellectual history of the West is Karl Marx (1818–1883), and his claim that religion is "the opium of the people" is among the most recognized of his assertions. Earlier in the text where the "opium" quote appears, he observes that religion is a human creation, a social product. In his words:

> *Man makes religion,* religion does not make man. . . . This state, this
> society, produce religion. . . . Religion is the sigh of the oppressed
> creature, the heart of a heartless world, just as it is the spirit of a
> spiritless situation. It is the *opium* of the people. . . . Religion is
> only the illusory sun which revolves round man as long as he does
> not revolve round himself.[11]

For Marx, religion was a secondary institution within society and a
consequence of the foundation (what he referred to as the "base") of
the social order, which for him was economics. His treatment of religion, thus, very clearly fits in the functional category. Religion exists
to serve a social function, which for Marx was to deaden the pain of
existence for the oppressed and suppress resistance in those who
might otherwise oppose the economic order.

Where Marx's characterization of religion is something less than
a systematic definition, another major contributor to the academic
study of religion, Emile Durkheim (1858–1917), presents his understanding as an explicit definition. As he writes in one of the classic
academic studies of religion, *The Elementary Forms of Religious Life:*

> A religion is a unified system of beliefs and practices relative to
> sacred things, that is to say, things set apart and forbidden—beliefs
> and practices which unite into one single moral community called a
> Church, all those who adhere to them. . . . [B]y showing that the
> idea of religion is inseparable from that of the Church, it makes it
> clear that religion should be an eminently collective thing.[12]

Like Marx's understanding, Durkheim's definition is functional in
character. For him, religion is necessarily collective, based in society,
and unifying of society. The function of religion is to unify society
into a collective whole. This is achieved through "beliefs and practices" (we could say, *myths* and *rituals*) that form a unified system
and, in turn, unite believers into a community. So, again, like Marx,
Durkheim understands religion as serving the needs of society.

Another important contributor to the academic study of religion,
Joachim Wach (1898–1955) offers an understanding of what religion
is in the context of his method of studying it. Like other studies
before and since, early on in his *Sociology of Religion,* Wach observes
that "[a]n examination of definitions of religion is beyond our
scope."[13] He then cites the one offered by another major scholar of
religion, Rudolf Otto, as the "most workable one": "Religion is the
experience of the Holy."[14] Otto's definition is substantive (defining
what religion *is* as opposed to what it *does*), but the content is a bit
ambiguous. What, after all, is "the Holy" and what counts as experience? Otto's famous work on the subject, *The Idea of the Holy*[15] seeks

to answer these very questions. Otto's theory is, however, a bit beyond our scope, but, for many (like Wach), his definition remains a "most workable one." To make it work, however, one must either follow Otto's theory or explicate the ambiguous terms. What makes Wach's understanding helpful is his explication of the term *experience* relative to religion.

For Wach, religious experience takes three major forms: theoretical (myths and teachings), practical (rituals and practices), and sociological (polity and group dynamics).[16] Using these three forms, Wach develops his interpretation of religion. Not so much a strict definition, Wach's approach presents an understanding of religion based on the major categories of religious experience. These categories supply the parameters of what religion is for him. Although predicated on Otto's substantive definition, Wach's interpretation is best classified as formal because he predicates the categories on a "comprehensive empirical, phenomenological, and comparative study."[17]

The most recent of the classic definitions presented here is that of Clifford Geertz (1926–2006). Like the others, Geertz's definition is frequently encountered in academic studies of religion, perhaps more often than the others, and typically in texts that consider definitions of religion. For Geertz, religion is defined in the context of culture, and for him, culture "denotes an historically transmitted pattern of meanings embodied in symbols, a system of inherited conceptions expressed in symbolic form by means of which men communicate, perpetuate, and develop their knowledge about and attitudes toward life."[18] Building on his primary conception of culture as a symbol system, religion for Geertz is:

(1) a system of symbols which acts to (2) establish powerful, pervasive, and long-lasting moods and motivations in men by (3) formulating conceptions of a general order of existence and (4) clothing these conceptions with such an aura of factuality that (5) the moods and motivations seem uniquely realistic.[19]

He further adds, importantly, that the study of religion focuses on "an analysis of the system of meanings embodied in the symbols which make up the religion proper, and . . . the relating of these systems to social structural and psychological processes."[20]

Geertz's definition is essentially functionalist in character, although it begins with a substantive assertion. In understanding religion, for him, it is important to recognize that it is (like culture as a whole) most fundamentally a system of symbols. That he specifies religion (substantively) as a system of symbols is noteworthy and one of Geertz's unique achievements, but the real energy of the definition is in what this system does—that is, how it functions. The specific system of symbols that is definitive of religion serves as a force within culture that establishes human "moods and motivations" (outlooks and dispositions to action). This power is derived from the symbol-system's capacity to create "an aura of factuality" around its conceptions of reality, thus legitimating the outlooks and dispositions it engenders. In brief, religion is the specific system of symbols that is most critical in the symbol-system of culture as a whole, for it is the web of religious symbols that stabilizes human existence and establishes reality itself.

In addition to these classic definitions, countless others could be considered. However, few would equal these in terms of their effectiveness or their frequency of citation in other sources. Turning now to the work of contemporary scholars allows exposure to other ways of defining religion. Since the classic definitions were largely functional in character (aside from those of Otto and Wach), the remainder of this section will consider representative substantive and formal definitions. First the substantive, of which an especially good example is found in the work of Bruce:

> Religion . . . consists of beliefs, actions, and institutions which assume the existence of supernatural entities with powers of action, or impersonal powers or processes possessed of moral purpose.[21]

Bruce advances this definition as one "that fits with broad contemporary common-sense reflection on the matter," which "seems to encompass what ordinary people mean when they talk of religion."[22]

Will Deming offers a succinct substantive definition: Religion is an "orientation to ultimate reality."[23] Deming also distinguishes between religion and religions, with the latter defined as "symbolic systems ('traditions') that provide a means for such orientations."[24] Readers will notice a similarity between Deming's definition of "religion" and Otto's, and his definition of "religions" with Geertz's notion of religion as a symbol system.

Catherine Albanese also includes the concept of a symbol system in her "descriptive statement":

> Religion . . . can be seen as *a system of symbols (creed, code, cultus) by means of which people (a community) locate themselves in the world with reference to both ordinary and extraordinary powers, meanings, and values.*[25]

Earlier in the same work, *America: Religion and Religions,* following her explication of the three types of definitions, Albanese observed that the approach taken in the book related to "the discipline of the history of religions, and so its understanding of religion is formal," and since it was also "about 'plain' religious history and likewise open to sociological and anthropological categories, its understanding is functional."[26]

Another good example of a formal description of religion is Ninian Smart's specification of seven dimensions of religion. As presented in *The World's Religions*, the dimensions are as follows:

1. Practical and Ritual
2. Experiential and Emotional
3. Narrative or Mythic
4. Doctrinal and Philosophic
5. Ethical and Legal
6. Social and Institutional
7. Material[27]

Smart's approach is not unlike Wach's. Where Wach offered three major *forms* (which are further unpacked to include additional features), Smart presents seven *dimensions*. In both instances, the scholars are interested in finding features that are characteristic of all religions, and that allow for the systematic study of individual religions, as well as comparative studies of two or more religions. Also, like Wach, Smart's approach reveals that formal approaches often focus on functional features. Although most of Smart's dimensions are related to Wach's forms, Smart's inclusion of the material dimension appears unique. In this area, Smart refers to "buildings, works of art, and other creations," including "those natural features of the world which are singled out as being of special sacredness and meaning."[28]

As noted previously, the selection of definitions presented here is designed to introduce readers to some of the classic understandings of religion and expose them to various ways in which religion has been academically defined. Its intent has also been to offer a context for the provisional description of religion, which will now be presented.

A Provisional Description of Religion

The classic definitions presented in the previous section have each influenced the provisional description offered here. The description itself is essentially formal, in Albanese's sense of the term (presented earlier), although it contains substantive elements and functional features as well. It is nonreductionistic insofar as it acknowledges the reality of a sacred realm as an object of human intending, which is not necessarily reducible to prior categories or conditions. The other theoretic issues dealt with in this primer are related to this provisional description:

> Religion is about power. It mediates our relationship with the source(s) of ultimate (sacred) power by suggesting, teaching, or commanding (1) a *belief* that the ultimate truth and meaning of human life is derived from and related to an order and purpose based on or decreed by the Ultimate (sacred) Power (e.g., gods, God, nature, cosmic principles, social order). (2) This belief is necessarily shared by a group or *community*. (3) This belief is *maintained* because of (A) the community's participation in certain special and uniquely patterned actions either personal or communal, typically called *rituals,* and (B) special (numinous) narratives, typically called *myths*, which deal with unique persons and/or events related to the sacred concerns and elements. (4) This belief in the foundational truth and meaning of human life is understood by participants in the religion to allow them (as individuals and as a community) a certain degree of *power over material conditions* (insofar as they live and act in harmony with the ultimate power) and to supply them with *answers to ultimate questions* regarding nature and the human condition (such as death, the afterlife, evil, one's place in society, why one succeeds or fails).

Of special note here is the character and function of myths and rituals. Myths are narratives about the sacred and humanity's relationship to the sacred. Typically, these narratives are set in a primordial time of origins and depict the actions and teachings of venerated ancestors, heroes, saviors, and gods. These actions and teachings both disclose the foundational reality of life and articulate the relationship of the believer to this reality. For the believer, myths communicate truths of such profundity that they cannot be doubted—truths that are so fundamental that even in the face of falsifying material and/or historical evidence, the believer accepts the reality of the myth. To the degree that myth loses its radical truthfulness, it loses its primary religious function.

Myths can be divided into three classes: meta, secondary, and tertiary.[29] The meta-myth is the master story of a culture, which articulates "the true motivating and psychological foundations of [a] civilization . . . expressions of the very being of the collective and universal civilization in which we are living."[30] Secondary and tertiary myths are narratives that offer more accessible versions of meta-myth, serving to personalize, vivify, and make it immediately relevant to individuals. In their secondary and especially their tertiary forms, myths guide and motivate religious activities. In their most formal sense, such activities are called *rituals.*

The general properties of rituals, as summarized by Sally F. Moore and Barbara G. Myerhoff, form the basis for the understanding of the term as it is used here. Moore and Myerhoff identify six properties of rituals:

1. *Repetition*
2. *Acting* (as in a play)
3. *Special behavior or stylization* (in actions or through the use of symbols)
4. *Order* (they are organized events at "prescribed times and places," "having a beginning and an end")
5. *Evocative presentational style; staging* (they "produce at least an attentive state of mind, and often an even greater commitment of some kind . . . through manipulation of symbols and sensory stimuli")
6. *The collective dimension* (they have "social meaning" and carry "a social message")[31]

I would nuance this understanding by noting that although rituals are often collective, they may certainly be performed by individuals privately. Most importantly, to these general properties, I would add that those rituals that are specifically *religious* have a sacred dimension—a sacred meaning and message as well as a social meaning and message. In fact, in many religions, especially those of antiquity, the sacred meaning/message is self-same with the social meaning/message. For the believer, rituals are the formal processes through which religious reality is experienced as one participates in or otherwise affirms a proper relationship to the sacred. In this regard, the "texts" that religious rituals follow are the myths of the religion, since these are the narratives that articulate the sacred realm and humanity's relationship with that realm.

In a religious sense, then, rituals and myths are intertwined in such a way that rituals reenact myths and myths illuminate rituals. Through rituals, the believer experiences the sacred realm described in myths and is brought into communion with the foundational reality of life. In a practical sense, the interrelation of myth and ritual is revealed in the relationship between mythic narratives such as the Exodus story and the ritual of Passover; the narrative of the Last Supper and the ritual of communion; or the narrative of the Buddha's enlightenment and the ritual of meditation. There is, thus, a dynamic nexus when the sacred reality disclosed in myths is fully experienced through the performance of rituals. In a study of New Year's festivals of the ancient world, Mircea Eliade uses the term *mythico-ritual* to characterize this synergy.[32] For many scholars, numerous seemingly non-religious aspects of contemporary culture reveal this same sort of mythico-ritual dynamism (e.g., politics, spectator sports, consumerism, and holiday celebrations). This dynamism is especially evident when functional approaches are used.

Although healthy religions routinely reveal the positive dimension of the synergy of myths and rituals, it may also be reflected negatively, since the loss of plausibility for one may undermine the meaningfulness of the other. In other words, when believers begin to doubt either the radical truth of the myths or the re-creative power of the rituals, the religious significance of both may decline. On the one hand, doubting the truth of the myths leads to a weakening of the significance of rituals, just as doubt of the power of rituals causes a corresponding erosion in the plausibility of mythic verities. As such doubts become more widespread among participants, religious communities may decline. On the other hand, in some instances a ritual may persist even after a myth has lost its meaning, leading to the generation of new myths related to the ritual. A similar situation may occur in the case of a ritual losing its vitality and a myth generating new ritual expressions.

General Classifications of Religion

Building on the provisional description of religion offered here, a further specification will be helpful to the development of this account of the relationship between religion and culture. This specification identifies two general types of religion, although there are certainly many other good ways of classifying religion. Before considering the two general types to be used here, and to give context to these types, an overview of several more common approaches will be offered.

Some of the more typical classifications of religion are by geographic origins, historical periods, and types of ultimate power. Each of these approaches is valuable to the study of religion and culture, they seldom appear in isolation, and texts dealing with religion and culture typically make use of some or all of these classifications. That will certainly be the case here and, in various ways, each will figure in later portions of this book.

Classifications by geographic origins are often used to organize the religious traditions of the world, and through that tell us something about the natural environments and human communities in which specific religions emerged and developed. Like the other approaches, classifications by geographic origins are of benefit to both the comparative study of religions and the study of specific traditions.

One effective deployment of this approach organizes the world of religious origins into three major geo-cultural areas: East Asia, South Asia, and West Asia. The major religions of East Asia include Confucianism, Daoism, and Buddhism. Although Buddhism originated in South Asia, it could be argued that it emerged as a major world religion only when it took root in East and Southeast Asia. Indigenous religions, sub-traditions, and smaller groups can also be accounted for in this method. For example, Shinto, the indigenous religion of Japan, would be included among the religions of East Asia, and the Buddhist sub-tradition, Theravada, would be classified as Southeast Asian. Smaller, younger groups, such as Falun Gong in China and Aum Shinrikyo in Japan, would be considered East Asian using this system.

A similar method would be used with the religions of South Asia and West Asia. Significant traditions with origins in South Asia are Hinduism (and its multitude of variations),[33] Buddhism (which originated there), Jainism, and Sikhism. The three major religions of West Asia are (in order of historical emergence) Judaism, Christianity, and Islam. The ancient religion Zororastrianism is also reasonably included here, as well.

Obviously, this method can be greatly expanded and considerably specified. Other geographic areas could be included in an expansion of this method of organization:

Africa

The Arabian Peninsula (Southwest Asia)

The Mediterranean Basin

Mesoamerica

Mesopotamia

North America

Northern Europe

South America and the Caribbean[34]

Historical periods are also used to classify religions. As early as elementary school, students are exposed to the organization of history into distinct periods. Perhaps the most familiar is the three-fold division into ancient, medieval, and modern. Although this is a rather basic division, it is based on the same general principle as more complex organizational models—that human history can be organized into distinct periods that can be distinguished from other similarly distinct periods. Contained in this general principle is the notion that, on the whole, cultural features throughout a given period are generally similar and that they are markedly *dissimilar* from cultural features of other periods.

The periodization of history is a fascinating topic, and there is a wide variety of schemes for specifying historical periods. When used to classify and analyze religions, historical periods serve to locate religion in terms of the culture of a specific time and place and relate religion to other significant events of that time and place. Less concerned with the physical environment than the geographic approach, the historical approach is interested in helping us understand religion in terms of cultural environments that are characteristic of distinct historical periods, and perhaps also in helping us gain insight into how religion in one period compares and contrasts with religion in other periods. The historical method certainly allows for the comparative study of religions and individual religions in a particular period. It also allows for the comparative study of a single religion in different historical periods. The periodization of history used in this primer identifies five distinct periods: ancient, classical, medieval, modern, and postmodern. It also recognizes important turning points in history, such as the Agricultural Revolution, the Axial Age, and the Enlightenment.

Yet another method of classifying religions is based on the nature of their ultimate power. Perhaps best known in the West is the distinction between monotheism and polytheism. Like the tripartite division of history, this basic sort of classification is helpful in a general sense, but in more detailed studies of religion, it is somewhat problematic, for a number of reasons. First, there are varieties of monotheism and disagreement about what is meant by the term itself. Trinitarian monotheisms are different from unitarian monotheisms. Monotheisms with incarnations are different from monotheisms without incarnations, and monotheisms in which the deity is an apersonal cosmic principle are different from monotheisms in which the deity is anthropomorphized in one way or another. Henotheisms, in which there is a supreme god above other gods, are sometimes understood as monotheisms, as are polytheisms in which a universal principle of being is conceptualized as a deity. These are some of the major challenges that complicate a simple monotheism–polytheism distinction.

More exacting classifications by ultimate power, thus, offer more specific terms for different types of ultimate power. Some of these terms are of assistance in clearing up the ambiguities noted above. For example, a distinction can be made between *monotheism* (a belief in a single god) and *monism* (a belief in a single supreme principle). The concept of *henotheism,* just noted, also helps clarify matters. Also of general assistance is the concept of *animism,* which refers to the belief that all things in nature are ensouled. It is sometimes conflated with polytheism. Also distinct from polytheism and somewhat related to animism is the notion of *mana,* a vital and impersonal life-force indwelling all creation, but present in varying degrees of intensity depending on the significance of the particular creation. Finally, *totemism* refers to the belief that a particular plant or animal is of ultimate importance to a particular community. Totemic systems are not polytheisms, although (like animism and the notion of mana) they are sometimes conflated with polytheism.

Besides these distinctions, many others could be made between concepts of ultimate power in different religious traditions and even sub-traditions of the same religion. In Christianity, for example, the ultimate power in one branch of the religion (Catholicism) involves a relationship between the Holy Spirit, God the Father, and Jesus that is different from their relationship in another (the Orthodox tradition). Is this the same ultimate power? The God of the Torah at times seems different than the God of the Quran, and different again from the God who appears in the New Testament. Is the Dao of Confucianism the same as the Dao of Daoism? Is the Buddha a man or a god? These and numerous other questions are relevant to classifications that seek to organize religions by types of ultimate power.

If we are going to classify religion according to concepts of ultimate power, details about the distinctions between the concepts are necessary and are necessarily determined by the depth of the study. The more basic the study, the more basic the distinctions; the more detailed the study, the more detailed the distinctions.

The Two General Types of Religion

Being a primer, this text will use a rather basic distinction between religions. It is a type of ultimate power classification, similar to those reviewed at the close of the last section. Although the distinction offered here is rudimentary, it is offered as an effective, workable method of organizing general inquiries and analyses of religion and culture. It is also one that allows for considerable expansion in detail and specificity, making it the base for more complex inquiries.

The basic distinction recognizes two general types of religion. The covering terms characterizing these two general types are *cosmological* and *transcendental.* As they are being used here, these terms were first introduced in the work of Eric Voegelin,[35] although the understanding and deployment of the terms in this work differ somewhat from Voegelin's original usage.

In brief, *cosmological* refers to religions and cultural systems that locate the ultimate power in the natural world. *Transcendental* refers to religions and/or cultural systems that locate the ultimate power in a supernatural dimension—literally, a realm beyond and radically different from nature. In addition, these systems affirmed a relationship (explained in various ways) between the ultimate power and human beings. For this reason, these transcendental systems are also characterized as *anthropological.*

As will be explored in more detail in Chapter 2, the transcendental religions are latecomers to the world stage, emerging in their earliest forms in the Axial Age (800–200 BCE)[36] and not attaining significant cultural power in the West until early in the Common Era. With the rise of transcendental religions came a corresponding decline in cosmological religious systems, which affirmed the ultimate power to be, in various expressions, Nature itself or derived from nature. The last great cosmological empire in the West was the Roman Empire.

Today, transcendental religions dominate the world, although it must be noted that there are few purely transcendental religions; most include some cosmological features, and it is perhaps best to conceive of the transcendental religions as a continuum, ranging from those with few cosmological features to those with many (or particularly notable) cosmological features. Constructing a model of such a continuum would be an interesting exercise, although beyond the immediate interests of this text.

For now, we can note that the major transcendental systems include those cited and briefly analyzed earlier in this chapter—all the major, global religions (and their subgroups), with the exception of various types of rather classical cosmological religiosity found in Hinduism. Transcendental religions, thus, include the two largest religions in the world, Christianity and Islam, along with Buddhism, Sikhism, and Judaism. Forms of Hinduism that stress transcendental notions (e.g., monism, Brahman as the cosmic principle, nondualism [Advaita], and the unitive oneness of Atman and Brahman) would be included in this category. Also included would be expressions of philosophical Daoism. Again, it must be noted that, in practice, none of these religions is purely transcendental, although some are much more so than others, and various subgroups may be markedly transcendental. However, as a general principle, these traditions affirm an openness to the infinite and a supernatural ultimate power.

Before the rise of these new religions, human religiosity (in fact, all of human culture) was cosmological. In such systems the sacred was immanent in the world and encountered in the context of nature: the flight of the sun and journey of the stars, the ebb and flow of seasons, the rise and fall of rivers, the cycles of the moon. There was no intrinsic separation between humans and the natural world that sustained life; so, too, was there no distinction between the social order and the order of the cosmos itself. Life was a continuous harmony. Religion and the other institutions of society were not independent entities, and that which we have identified as culture (the human-made world) was a manifestation of the sacred and integrated into the grand order of the cosmos.

Such religions served to mediate the relationship between human beings and the awesome and enchanted cosmos. They articulated the sacredness of places, objects, power spots, holy mountains, sacred groves, totems, male sky gods and female gods of the earth; their festivals were celebrations of the earth and its bounty; their myths were stories of ancestors and heroes who exemplified the norms of humanity's relationship with the divine; their rituals celebrated this relationship in the context of nature's ceaseless cycles. The changing of seasons was of sacred significance for everyone and needed the religious attention of the entire culture. Likewise, the ending of droughts was a cause for collective sacrifice, a prosperous harvest was an occasion for massive culturewide celebrations, and planting seasons were marked with fertility rituals.

Unlike religions of the contemporary West, which are discrete institutions, these religions were collective enterprises based on deeply rooted cultural beliefs about the order and process of the cosmos and humanity's right relationship with it. With the order and process of the cosmos as the ground of sacred meaning, religion served as the source and force of legitimation and guidance for culture and human activity relative to the sacred ground. Rather than standing apart from the rest of culture, ancient cosmological religion was embedded in its midst, sacralizing its political and economic processes and cosmicizing its social structures. Myths were universal in intent, and rituals were collective. Through them, religion affirmed and acted out the truth of the cosmic order that was already revealed in everyday life, sacralizing culture and sanctifying the social order. This truth was that the way things *are* is the way they ought to be. These were religions structured for a world we do not know today and can hardly even imagine. It was an enchanted world—and the specific world that began to be disenchanted with the rise of transcendental religions.

Cosmological religion goes by many names today: naturalism, animism, primal, archaic, Paganism, Neopaganism, and Wicca. In its most widespread and culturally dominant expression it is probably best known as *polytheism.* It was this type of religion that flourished in the last great cosmological culture of the West, the Roman Empire. Of course, the institutional polytheism of the Graeco-Roman world was eventually overcome and eradicated by what would become the largest religion in the world—Christianity.

The background and consequences of this conquest will be considered in the next chapter. From this point on, the focus of this text will be primarily on Western (Euro-American) culture and the approach largely historical.

Endnotes

1. See Peter Berger, *The Sacred Canopy: Elements of a Sociological Theory of Religion* (Garden City, NY: Anchor Books, 1969), 6–7; Bruce David Forbes, "Introduction" in *Religion and Popular Culture in America,* ed. Forbes and Jeffrey H. Mahan, 2nd ed. (Berkeley, CA: University of California Press, 2005), 2; and H. Richard Niebuhr, *Christ and Culture* (New York: Harper & Row, Harper Torchbooks, 1951), 32 ff.
2. *Webster's New Collegiate Dictionary,* 8th ed., sv. "culture," 5a.
3. Berger, 3. Here as elsewhere, when linguistic sexism appears in the quoted material, it is not altered in this text.
4. Clifford Geertz, "Religion as a Cultural System," in *Reader in Comparative Religion: An Anthropological Approach,* ed. William Lessa and Evon Z. Vogt, 3rd ed. (New York: Harper and Row, 1972), 168.
5. Darrell J. Fasching and Dell deChant, *Comparative Religious Ethics: A Narrative Approach* (Oxford, UK: Blackwell, 2001), 17.
6. Steve Bruce, *Religion in the Modern World: From Cathedrals to Cults* (Oxford, UK: Oxford University Press, 1996), 6.
7. Ibid., 7.
8. Daniel L. Pals, *Eight Theories of Religion,* 2nd ed. (New York: Oxford University Press, 2006), 12–13.
9. Catherine L. Albanese, *America: Religions and Religion,* 4th ed. (Belmont, CA: Thomson Wadsworth, 2007), xiii.
10. "Definition" is used very broadly here. Besides strict, systematic definitions, it includes general understandings, descriptions, and claims about the essence of religion.
11. Karl Marx, *Contribution to the Critique of Hegel's Philosophy of Right* (1844), as cited in Reinhold Niebuhr, *Marx and Engels on Religion* (New York: Schocken Books, 1964), 41–42. Italics in the original text.
12. Emile Durkheim, *The Elementary Forms of Religions Life,* trans. Joseph Ward Swain (New York: The Free Press/Macmillan, 1915), 62–63.

13. Joachim Wach, *Sociology of Religion* (Chicago: University of Chicago Press, 1971), 13.
14. Ibid. See also Rudolf Otto, *The Idea of the Holy,* trans. John H. Harvey (London: Oxford University Press, 1982).
15. See Otto, as cited in n.14.
16. Wach, 19–34.
17. Ibid., 15.
18. Clifford Geertz, as cited in Walter Capps, *Religious Studies: The Making of a Discipline* (Minneapolis: Fortress Press, 1995), 180.
19. Geertz, "Religion as a Cultural System," 168.
20. Ibid., 178.
21. Bruce, 7.
22. Ibid.
23. Will Deming, *Rethinking Religion: A Concise Introduction* (New York: Oxford University Press, 2005), 15.
24. Ibid., 146.
25. Albanese, 9. Passage is in italics in Albanese's work.
26. Ibid., xiii.
27. Ninian Smart, *The World's Religions,* 2nd ed. (Cambridge, UK: Cambridge University Press, 1998), 13–22.
28. Ibid., 21.
29. The specification of three classes of myth is derived, with some modifications, from Jacques Ellul. My meta-myth corresponds to what Ellul refers to as the "basic" or "essential" myth of a culture. My designation of secondary and tertiary myths is derived from Ellul, although, in my deployment, the two are more precisely distinguished from each other. See Jacques Ellul, *The New Demons* (New York: Seabury Press, 1975), 88–121, esp. 100–110.
30. Ibid., 109.
31. For more detail, see Sally F. Moore and Barbara G. Myerhoff, "Introduction: Secular Ritual," in Moore and Myerhoff, ed., *Secular Ritual* (Amsterdam, The Netherlands: Van Gorcum, Assen, 1977), 7–8. Terms in italics and quoted material in parentheses are Moore and Myerhoff's.
32. For example, see Eliade's usage of the term in *Cosmos and History: The Myth of the Eternal Return* (New York: Harper Torchbooks, 1959), 68–70.
33. *Hinduism* is here recognized as a general term for the vast (and widely differing) religions of India. Derived from "Hindu," a term applied by outsiders (first Muslims and later the British) to residents of the Indian subcontinent, it is a convenient, although hardly precise, term for beliefs that range from cosmological polytheisms to transcendental monisms.

34. These are but a sampling. The use of geographic origins for purposes of classification is essentially limited only by the limits of distinct geographic locales in which specific religious communities originated and the interests of specialists. Additional geographic areas might include the sub-Arctic, Pacific Island groups (Melanesia, Micronesia, and Polynesia), Australia, Central Asia, and specific nations, such as Japan and the United States.

35. Voegelin used these terms to distinguish between two ways of understanding culture and human existence. See Eric Voegelin, *The New Science of Politics* (Chicago: University of Chicago Press, 1952); and *Israel and Revelation* (Baton Rouge: Louisiana State University Press, 1956).

36. See Karl Jaspers, *The Origin and Goal of History* (London: Routledge, 1953), 51ff.

2

The Axial Age: Transcendental Religions and Those They Replaced

As noted in the previous chapter, the transcendental religions are new arrivals on the cultural stage, with their origin being traced to the Axial Age (800–200 BCE). Their success has been so complete and far-reaching that today common-sense understandings of religion often extend no further than religions of this type, and even scholarly approaches may use definitions that restrict its meaning to include only these transcendental religions.

To better understand the transcendental religions, this chapter will review their historical emergence in a number of distinct cultures. It will also consider the cosmological religions of antiquity, both to highlight their contrast with the transcendental religions that eclipsed them and also because the structure of these religions may tell us much about the relationship of religion and culture in the contemporary world. Finally, this chapter will offer a brief explication of the concept of disenchantment and its relationship to the transcendental religions.

The Axial Age: Visionaries, Beliefs, and Structures

The notion of an Axial (or Axis) Age was introduced by Karl Jaspers (1883–1969), in *The Origin and Goal of History* (1949), to characterize the 600-year period from 800 to 200 BCE.[1] During this time, religious visionaries from different parts of Eurasia began affirming that the ground of being and source of ultimate power was *transcendental* (transcendent of nature) and *supernatural*. In addition, these visionaries and the religious systems that developed on the basis of their teachings and those of their followers affirmed a relationship (explained in various ways) between the ultimate power and human beings. For this reason, the transcendental systems are also characterized as *anthropological*. In the West, the anthropological element in transcendental religions is best revealed in the notion of an eternal soul. In these systems there is, thus, a supernatural dimension to the human as well as the ultimate power; in fact, this supernatural dimension (the soul) is recognized as the key to humanity's openness to the infinite and the very essence of human beings.

Over time, the claims of many of these visionaries were systematized into religions, and religious communities with myths and rituals based on their claims developed—many of which continue to this day. It is striking how many major visionaries were active during the Axial Age. In this period, in South Asia, transcendental notions appeared in a collection of teachings called the Upanishads. Among these teachings (later recorded in written texts) one finds religious ideals frequently associated with Hinduism—especially in the West. These include the concept of an ultimate power, *Brahman,* which is universally present yet isolated in no single thing. Brahman pervades all creation, including the spaces between the things, and the spaces between the spaces. The Upanishads witness the anthropological dimension of transcendental religions in their affirmation that the innermost essence of humans *(atman)* is one with and part of Brahman. They further affirm the religious ideal of liberation from the physical material world and the cycle of reincarnation *(samsara)* through the fully conscious union of atman with Brahman.

Also in South Asia during the Axial Age, two major visionaries amplified the transcendental religious teachings of the Upanishads while simultaneously challenging the existing social order. These visionaries were Mahavira (540–468 BCE), who founded Jainism, and Siddhartha Gautama (the Buddha) (550–480 BCE). Both Jainism and Buddhism rejected the rigid hierarchical organization of the caste system and the religious institutions of Brahmanism, through which a priestly caste (the Brahmins) controlled religion. Both articulated the ideal of freedom from the fetters of matter and samsara; and both stressed compassion and non-violence *(ahimsa),* with Jainism being the more exacting of the two. They do differ in the notion of the human essence, with Jainism recognizing the presence of a soul *(jiva)* in all things and Buddhism rejecting such an essence in its concepts of the *skandahs* (five "aggregates" of existence that combine to create the illusion of a self) and *anatman* (no-atman). Once freed from samsara, in Jainism, the jiva ascends to the apex of the universe, and in Buddhism, *nirvana* ensues—bliss, the end of rebirth, infinite perception.

China at this time also produced two great visionaries: Confucius (551–479 BCE) and Lao Tze (circa 6th century BCE). Confucius proposed a new cultural order based on the harmonization of society according to ideal patterns in human relationships, including *ren* (harmony) and *li* (proper rites and ceremonies). Ren functions somewhat like "the good" in Platonic idealism—that is, it is a grand transcendental ideal, which is sought by those who are enlightened and (hopefully) the leaders of society. Lao Tze, the mythic founder of what we today call Daoism, is credited with a system that recognizes a universal principle (the Dao) that transcends all immediate expressions and yet pervades all of nature. The Dao is understood as the ever-moving, ever-vital interrelationship of seeming opposites (yin and yang). It can be experienced by humans even if it cannot be fully understood. It is beyond reason but lies at the very heart of creation.

In Persia, Zoroaster (630–553 BCE), the "mythic" founder of what we today call Zoroastrianism, affirmed a cosmic dualism. His conception of the universe was based on an eternal struggle between Ahura Mazda (the ruler of the universe, who represents all that is good) and Ahriman (an evil spirit, who represents all that is opposed to the good). Together with their spiritual associates, the two are locked in a struggle that transpires throughout all of creation. The role of humans in this process is to align themselves with Ahura Mazda and the forces of good. The struggle will eventually cease with the victory of Ahura Mazda, after a final cataclysmic battle at the end of time. In the aftermath of this apocalyptic battle, the souls of all humanity will face a final judgment, and those deemed worthy will live eternally in a new and purified world. Many scholars recognize Zoroastrianism as a major influence on early Judaism and the root tradition for apocalypticism and afterlife beliefs in the Western monotheistic traditions.

In this period, Judaism as we know it today began to take form. The great temple in Jerusalem was destroyed, followed by the Babylonian Exile (587–538), and the Jewish prophets (most notably Ezekiel and Isaiah) articulated a transcendental monotheism. This is quite evident in the opening of the book of Ezekiel. The Axial Age saw the Torah take written form and in subsections (such as the "Elohistic" and "Priestly" sources) offer conceptions of an ultimate power as a transcendental and singular deity—a universal God who made the cosmos, and dwells beyond it, yet influences human events. Prophetic works of this period include apocalyptic elements and, in Isaiah especially, messianic concepts are introduced.

During the Axial Age in Greece, the Western philosophic tradition was born, first in the work of the pre-Socratic philosophers such as Thales (624–545), Heraclitus (540–475), and Democritus (460–370), and later with Socrates (470–399), Plato (428–347), and finally Aristotle (384–322). Not unlike the religious visionaries previously noted, these thinkers asked questions about the meaning of existence, the order of society, and the nature of the world. They sought answers based on rational inquiry and critical analysis. Importantly, they looked beyond the existing cosmological polytheism of their culture for answers to their questions about the cosmos, the meaning of life, and the social order. In addition, as they looked beyond the cosmological worldview to formulate their understandings, they frequently looked back at it and the religions that supported it with disdain, disparagement, and dismay.

The Greek philosophers' rejection and critique of cosmological religious explanations is a common feature in all of the Axial Age religions. What was uncommon about their approach (as well as that of Confucius) was that the new understandings they expressed were largely non-religious in character. Unlike the Greeks (aside from Plato, perhaps), the other visionaries of the period challenged the existing religious systems of their day on the basis of new conceptions about the cosmos and human existence that were either intrinsically religious or quickly acquired religious features. In other words, the Axial Age witnessed the beginning of a religious revolution, a struggle against the prevailing myths, rituals, community structures, and conceptions of ultimate power that dominated and legitimated the societies in which they emerged. The religious revolution of the Axial Age, thus, was also a social revolution, and one that eventually affected all of human culture.

What were once called the Great World Religions (Hinduism, Buddhism, Judaism, Christianity, and Islam) grew out of the transcendental worldview of the Axial Age. This worldview held that the ultimate power is radically different from and beyond the world of nature. Relative to this new ultimate power, the old cosmological gods of nature were typically treated in one of three ways:

1. They were reduced to secondary, intermediate, or only locally significant beings.

2. They were ignored, treated as non-existent, or dismissed as naive superstitions; belief in such beings being seen as perhaps a mistake in understanding, childish, or simplemindedness.

3. The cosmological deities were taken quite seriously and their existence recognized as a direct challenge to the new transcendental systems. In its most radical expression, this approach identified the old gods as manifestations of actual evil.

The first two approaches are typically those found in the transcendental religions of South and East Asia. The third approach is largely restricted to the transcendental monotheistic religions that emerged in West Asia (Judaism, Christianity, and Islam), although they certainly excelled in their use of the first two approaches as well.

With the rise of transcendental religions, the archaic[2] cosmological religious system of temple-sacrifice-priest began to be replaced with a new system of community-study/prayer-teacher. In archaic cosmological cultures, ritual activity occurred at unique (sacred) locations, generally referred to as temples. Ritual activities that occurred were chiefly sacrificial in character. Commodities of value (agricultural and dairy products, animals, and on rare occasions, persons) were offered to the gods. The rituals of sacrifice were conducted by a trained class of specialists, the priests. Those who were not of the priestly class were forbidden to perform the rituals. They would not know how to properly perform the sacrifice, which would show disrespect to the gods, the sacrifice, and the priests. Moreover, it was simply not their social role. This model of religious activity is reflected with a fair degree of uniformity in pre-Axial archaic cultures.

In contrast to this model, beginning in the Axial Age, the transcendental religions developed a new approach to the practice of religion, one very much in keeping with their conceptions of ultimate power and the anthropological principles they affirmed. Replacing the place-bound temple as the locus of religious activity was the notion of a community of believers. The center of the religion became not a place, but a group of people joined together by a shared belief. In their earliest expressions, these transcendental groups were social outsiders, communities whose beliefs and practices were clearly different from those in the surrounding cosmological society. Notable examples of such communities would include the synagogue of Judaism, the sangha of Buddhism, and the ashram of Hinduism.

Where these people gathered was not nearly as important as why they gathered. And why they gathered was to learn the truth about the transcendental ultimate power, the world, and themselves—a truth that, again, was at odds with the truth of the culture as a whole. Study and religious practices based on this study (such as prayer and meditation), thus, became the basis for ritual activity in transcendental religions.

Finally, in place of a special class of specialists who performed rituals, the leader of the transcendental religious community functions as a teacher for the community. Rather than conducting sacrifices for others, the teacher explains the truth of existence, gives instruction for individual religious practice (prayer and meditation), and leads the community in collective expressions of those practices. Two classic examples of the transcendental religious leader are the guru in Hinduism and the rabbi in Judaism.

Before the Axial Age: The Cosmological Communities of Antiquity

Ancient cosmological religion took two general forms, primal and archaic. Both conform to the description of the cosmological religions of antiquity given in Chapter 1, insofar as nature functioned as the ultimate power, and religion served to integrate humans with the cosmos and their immediate community. In these systems, religion, per se, was indistinguishable from society as a whole; and although the primal and archaic differ in their social structures and material expressions, their sacralization of nature and society is essentially the same.

Key distinguishing features between the two systems can be traced to material developments in human culture with the deciding event being the first great agricultural revolution, beginning around 8000 BCE. Prior to this revolution, which allowed for the development of sedentary societies and vast increases in population, human communities were tribal, nomadic, and organized around the vital, all-consuming quest for sustenance. This quest served as the basis for the well-known "hunter-gatherer" socio-religious system, here distinguished as primal culture.

Primal Culture

In primal communities, the elemental threat and promise of nature were ever-present realities, and right relationship with the power of nature an ever-present concern. As with all ancient cosmological systems (including the archaic, to be presented later in the chapter) the meta-myth (master story) of primal communities told the story of nature and the right relationship of humans with it. More explicitly, it affirmed success and well-being in the context of the natural world, which was gained through a proper relationship with the forces of nature, and revealed in the maintenance of social (in this case, tribal) order and the fulfillment of social (tribal) duties by individuals.

Rather than discrete and individualized deities, primal communities articulated the sacredness of nature as what is generally termed *mana,* the mysterious power and potency present in all things—more present in some than others.[3] Beings and elements possessing considerable mana would be those that might bring great harm or benefit to the tribe: the thunder cloud or the bear, on the one hand, the gently flowing brook or the caribou herd on the other. Mythically, primal communities affirmed kinship with the sacred power of nature through narratives of hero-ancestors whose activities and right relationship with the forces of nature, and mana-rich beings and elements prefigured the ideal activities of their descendants. Ritually, primal communities sought to reenact the mythic experiences of their forebears, thereby, manifesting and possessing mana as had their ancestors.

The being with perhaps the greatest mana of all was the shaman; this was the religious specialist of the primal tribe, chosen not on the basis of heredity or class but rather on the basis of sensitivity to the sacred realm of natural powers and the mysteries of mana. He or she was the storyteller, the narrator of primal myths, the one who told of ancestors, the origins and order of the world, and the place of human beings in it. The shaman was also the healer, the visionary, the instructor. She or he would be consulted and give guidance regarding what was right and wrong to do, for the shaman knew the ways of mana and the proper manner to approach it and its manifestations. The directions of the shaman guided the community in ritual behavior: what needed to be done for the good of the tribe, where to hunt and gather, how to call the spirit of the animals, invoke the power of mana, initiate the young, and when to leave one locale for another.

Chief among the rituals were those related to transitions. In the human community, these rituals dealt with birth, puberty, old age, and death. But human transitions were not the only ones of concern to these communities. Equally important were transitions in the natural world: the mating, birth, and death of animals (especially those taken in the hunt); and the revival of plants in the spring, their fruiting, and their death in winter. Overarching all other transitions were the grand transitions of the cosmos itself; the wandering of planets and constellations across the heavens, the waxing and waning of the moon, and perhaps most critically, the changing of seasons. In primal communities, these transitions were matters of the gravest importance for life had to be lived in accord with the sacred norms of the cosmos. To miss or misunderstand these processes was to risk the disaster of disorder. Times and events of transition, therefore, required the greatest ritual attention so they might be experienced in ways consistent with the myths of the ancestors, respectful of the manifestations of mana, and in harmony with the order and processes of the cosmos.

As the primal gave way to the archaic, we do not see so much of a revolution as an increase in complexity, specialization, and individuation in the social forms and religious symbolism of humanity's relationship with the sacred. Nature remained the ultimate power and sacred ground of ultimate concern for nature was the source of all sustenance, and the basis of existence itself. At the material level, only the means of gaining nature's blessings changed—from foraging for edible vegetation to farming, from hunting animals to harvesting them and their by-products. The general mythic and ritual structures of archaic cultures remained essentially the same as those of primal cultures, with major modifications being the advent of the archaic religious structure sketched earlier (temple-sacrifice-priest) and a new way of conceptualizing the ultimate power—gods. As explained by Robert N. Bellah, in this system,

> mythical beings are more objectified, conceived as actively and sometimes willfully controlling the natural and human world, and as beings with whom men must deal in a definite and purposive way; in a word they have become gods.[4]

Still, the cosmological conception of human religious life continued as the norm. As Bellah observes:

> The individual and his society are seen as merged in a natural-divine cosmos. Traditional social structures and social practices are considered to be grounded in the divinely instituted cosmic order, and there is little tension between religious demand and social conformity. Indeed, social conformity is at every point reinforced with religious sanction.[5]

Archaic Culture

Although clearly discernible expressions of archaic culture are not present until around 3000 BCE, the roots of archaic culture can be traced back to around the Agricultural Revolution of 8000 BCE when animals and plants began to be domesticated. With the rise of large-scale agriculture and subsequent urbanization, history's earliest civilizations began to emerge, initially as city-states and later as widely extended empires. The earliest forms of these civilizations were located in the river valleys of eastern, south central, and western Asia, and along the Nile in north Africa. By the turn of the eras, this type of culture had come to dominance in large parts of China, South Asia, East Asia, and the Mediterranean Basin. Many centuries later, it emerged in Meso- and South America.

These new urban civilizations differed culturally from their primal precursors in numerous ways. Among the major innovations that occurred with the development of archaic culture were: rigid hierarchical class stratification, literacy (at least among the social elite), patriarchy, and institutional bureaucracy. What was once called the *rise of civilization* can now be seen as essentially a tracking of the increasing material and institutional sophistication in these archaic cultures.

First, of course, was the domestication of plants and animals, which led to population increases and sedentary communities; writing emerged soon after, along with the manufacture of ceramic vessels and textiles. Soon enough came bricks, mathematics, wheels, cities, accounting procedures, commerce, law codes, money, tombs for departed royalty, geometry, astronomy, sophisticated solar calendars, mastery of metals (bronze, then iron), and so on. The trajectory of material development and major innovations are relatively consistent cross-culturally during the archaic epoch, with some cultural systems advancing materially and technologically more rapidly than others at different times during the period.

In the religious sphere, however, the cosmological sense of the sacred remained virtually unchanged from the primal period. Religious innovations that did occur seem essentially contingent on sociological modifications brought on by urbanization and its attendant class stratification and individuation: the establishment of priest classes as part of the social hierarchy and the emergence of gods as individualized personifications of the sacred forces of nature or divine patrons of human activities dependent on nature. These changes tended to systematize, bureaucratize, and institutionalize the relationship of humanity to the sacred; but the sacred continued to be the force(s) of nature, and the meta-myth continued to be the story of nature and the right relationship of humans with it. And, again, more explicitly, it affirmed success and well-being in the context of the natural world, gained through a proper relationship with the forces of nature, and revealed in the maintenance of social order and the fulfillment of social (class/caste) duties by individuals.

Only with the transcendental revolution of the Axial Age did any substantial changes in religiosity occur, and even then, it took centuries for the new transcendental systems to influence archaic culture and even longer for them to eliminate large-scale expressions of cosmological religiosity. In this regard, the earliest possible date for a major and distinct influence of transcendental religion on archaic culture is perhaps no earlier than the third century BCE in East Asia, with Ashoka and Buddhism, and certainly no earlier than the late third or early fourth century CE in West Asia and the Mediterranean Basin, with the rise of Christianity. An argument could be made for the sixth century BCE, with Zoroastrianism in the Persian Empire, but a date for the transcendentalization of Central Asia is better linked to the rise of Islam. In fact, in its most fundamental characteristics, archaic religion was little different at the turn of the eras from what it was at the time of its emergence. It also varied little from one cultural system to another.[6]

In its general form, archaic religion's sacralization of nature and the cosmos was articulated as hierarchically stratified pantheons, in which various deities performed specialized functions, just as humans did in the archaic world's newly emerging urban centers. The gods were thus embodiments of nature, the ultimate power and sacred ground of being; so too were human beings, only on a smaller, less-significant scale. The myths of archaic cosmological cultures were narratives about these gods, their origins, their relationship with the order-process of the cosmos and human society, and their importance to the everyday lives of human beings. Each of the myths were variations on the meta-myth for each was contingent on the story of nature's sacred power and the right relationship of humans with it. To the degree that the myths concerned the exploits of the gods, they are secondary myths, insofar as the gods serve as representatives and personifications of the meta-myths. And to the degree that they relate to human beings, they are tertiary myths, insofar as they articulate the right relationship of humans to the sacred order.

Rituals were essentially economic transactions between the gods and individuals or entire communities; again, no different from the immediate social activities of persons and social classes in these times. Transactions with the sacred beings were mediated and directed by religious specialists (priests). These rituals generally involved the sacrifice of precious commodities (food and libations) to the gods at geographically discrete locales and/or mythically specified calendrical times when it was appropriate to express appreciation or address petitions to the deities. Although specific rituals varied widely, due to the specific desires of individuals and communities, their ultimate purpose was always the reestablishment of the right relationship between individuals and whole communities with the sacred realm.

The grandest rituals were those that occurred at the transition of seasons and years, when entire cultures would join in massive collective events celebrating the harmony of all creation and affirming a society's continuity with the sacred cosmos and its supervisors (the gods). In these rituals, the great myths were reenacted and the meta-myth revivified, thus affirming and assuring the regeneration of the cosmic cycle and bringing success and well-being for all.

Affinities and Continuities in Ancient Cosmological Cultures

With the rise of archaic religions, the primal notion of mana seems to have been replaced or translated into polytheistic pantheons. To a certain extent, this is precisely what happened, but only to the extent that the sacred had become personified as anthropomorphic deities, rather than generalized throughout the natural world and concentrated in sacred creatures and natural elements of considerable power. The gods were the forces of nature, individualized and personalized, to be sure, but still fundamentally expressions of nature's vast and awesome power. In short, the sacred force of nature became the god Uranus or Varuna; the thunderstorm became individualized as Zeus, Marduk, or Indra; the terrible disorder of war became Ares or Mars; the capriciousness of the oceans became Poseidon; and the mana of powerful animals became personified as the Sphinx (a lion god of Egypt and Greece), Ganesha (the elephant-headed god of India), or the Minotaur (the bull-headed guardian of the labyrinth of Minos and Greek culture as a whole).

Also, like their primal forebears, humans needed to know and maintain their proper relationship with the sacred cosmos. This relationship was articulated in myths and reaffirmed in ritual. Where primal societies had shamans to remember the myths and give guidance in ritual, archaic cultures had priests to guide ritual, and by the second millennium BCE, some also had written versions of their myths.[7] This led to a compartmentalization of religious activity. Unlike the shaman, the office of priest was highly specialized and those who filled the office often came from an hereditary priestly class. Individual deities would often have their own priesthood, and specific ritual tasks would be performed by priests specializing in those tasks. Also, unlike the shaman, who tended to be concerned with all aspects of the sacred life of the tribe, the role of the priest increasingly became focused on formal rituals conducted at discrete times and places, which typically involved sacrifice. Finally, due to literacy and the establishment of written texts, myths began to become standardized and no longer open to creative interpretations as was the case in primal, shamanistic cultures. Pantheons, priest-castes, and literacy did not, however, change the fundamental religious ecology of the cosmological community.

The sacred ground itself remained the same as it had always been: the natural world, the cosmos upon which human life depended entirely and without question. One's sacred duty remained the same as well: maintain the proper relationship with the mysterious and powerful forces of the natural world (whether as the manifestations of mana or in the personages of gods). Myths, of which creation myths most clearly expressed the meta-myth, disclosed the eternal cosmic context of the relationship; and rituals, of which seasonal rituals were the most wide-ranging and culturally extensive, allowed persons and whole cultures to reaffirm and literally reestablish the relationship. Nature, however it might be symbolized, was the ultimate power, the sacred ground of being, and as Bellah reminds us, "The individual and his society are seen as merged in a natural-divine cosmos . . . [in which] . . . social structures and social practices are considered to be grounded in the divinely instituted cosmic order, and there is little tension between religious demand and social conformity. Indeed, social conformity is at every point reinforced with religious sanction."[8] It was this "natural-divine cosmos" that was was rejected by the transcendental religions, first in the Axial Age, and later (and more thoroughly) by subsequent religions—most especially, Christianity and Islam.

The Principle and Process of Disenchantment in the West

Fundamental to this rejection of the sacredness of nature is the principle that Max Weber called "Entzauberung der Welt," the disenchantment of the world. It has long been argued that this disenchantment, or desacralization, has its roots in the first transcendental religion of West Asia—Axial Age Judaism.

Following Eric Voegelin, Weber, and others, Peter Berger presents an excellent sketch of the disenchantment process in terms of the scriptures and the religious traditions of ancient Israel.[9] The key to the process is the distinction between the religious system of early Judaism, which was transcendental in character, and the worldview of other cultures existing in the ancient Near East, which was cosmological in character. It was precisely the cosmological worldview of the indigenous cultures and great civilizations of the Near East that was challenged by the religion of ancient Israel, and it was their "world" that was in principle (although not in practice) disenchanted. The cultural energy of the disenchantment process, then, is to be found in the profound difference between the transcendental and cosmological approaches to life and meaning. As noted previously, cosmological religions locate the ground of being or ultimate power in the world of nature. In contrast, transcendental religions locate the ground of being in a supernatural dimension—literally, a realm beyond and radically different from nature. The process through which these two systems interacted in the West can now be considered in somewhat greater detail.

The eclipse of cosmological religion by transcendental systems began during the Axial Age, but it was not until the Christianization of Rome in the fourth century CE that the transcendental worldview became a large-scale cultural force in the West. These religions, of which Judaism was the first sustained expression in the West, recognize the highest meaning of life, the divine font of existence, the cause and principle of creation, in short, the foundation of ultimate concern as unnatural; beyond, above, and utterly different from the material, physical, terrestrial, and natural world. In addition, these religions affirm that humanity has some sort of relationship with this supernatural power, which in the monotheistic systems is called God, and this relationship in various ways legitimates humanity's dominion over nature.[10]

It is not just that the human essence (the soul) is supernatural, which is a feature of the anthropological component typical of transcendental systems, but that the relationship of humans to the ultimate power is such that human existence is recognized as superior to all other creations, and second only to God. Certainly, this arrangement also includes a recognition that, with their dominion, humans are also called to responsibility and stewardship over the rest of creation. While this is indeed so, dominion has generally trumped stewardship.

In the course of the development of the transcendental monotheisms, the cosmological gods themselves were condemned and the sacredness of natural elements (even nature itself) denied. This is what is meant by desacralization or disenchantment. What was once sacred is now ordinary; what was once enchanted is now mundane. Moreover, in many instances, what was sacred in cosmological religions, became evil for the transcendental religions of the West (e.g., gods, the sacralization of nature, the rituals of fertility and procreation).

As noted previously, the Western forms of transcendental religiosity (Judaism, Christianity, and Islam) have tended to be extremely hostile toward cosmological religions. Relativizing the natural order to the transcendent order, as in the opening chapter of Genesis or the Gospel of John, Western monotheism attacked the sacred reality of cosmological religion and rejected the legitimacy of its myths and rituals. The mythic background of this antagonism can be found in the Tanak (Old Testament) and its various narratives pitting the God of Israel against various nature deities, condemning "idol" worship, and celebrating the victorious struggles of Israelite heroes against their cosmological adversaries.

In practice, the assault on cosmological religion celebrated in the Tanak (Hebrew Bible), however, was relatively small-scale and short-lived. After all, ancient Israel was a small and relatively weak nation compared to the great cosmological empires of the period, and its challenge to the cosmological systems of its powerful neighbors was essentially rhetorical and restricted to its own sacred myths. Even during the period of its greatest power, ancient Israel struggled with cosmological religion within its own borders. Moreover, Judaism, as a transcendental religion, per se, really only emerged after the Exile, and, then, as a small, alternative religious community subsumed within world-dominant cosmological culture.

The situation changed dramatically with the rise of Christianity and, most emphatically, its acceptance as the religion of the Roman Empire. In Christianity (and later Islam), the monotheistic assault on cosmological religion ceased to be rhetorical and mythic, and became instead a matter of public policy and practice. Following Judaism, Christianity came on the historical scene bristling with critique and condemnation of the old cosmological systems, their gods and sacred orders, their shamans and priests, their myths and rituals. From subtle appropriation and reconstruction of myths and rituals to aggressive conversion campaigns and legal prohibitions against cosmological religious practices, the history of the rise of Christianity has included an aggressive and purposeful assault on cosmological religions. History has revealed it to have been enormously successful.

In summary, the transcendental worldview of the West, rooted in Biblical notions of transcendental monotheism, supernatural creation myths, and human dominion over nature, emerged in opposition to the cosmological systems of antiquity. As conceptualized under the heading of disenchantment, the new monotheistic myths served to desacralize the natural world and eviscerate cosmological religion. They denied and condemned its gods and the ambient sacredness of the cosmos by placing a single God above and beyond the cosmos, replacing the reverence for the cycles of nature with a reverence for history, and replacing the magical and mysterious potency of nature with a moral and rational God, who in the process of creating the world, elevated human beings above the rest of creation. In its earliest expressions, the monotheistic condemnation of cosmological religions was largely restricted to myth; with the rise of Christianity, however, it became a matter of public policy. As a result, the original and longest-lasting form of human religiosity was largely suppressed in Western culture. Although the concept of disenchantment is of great value to theoretic understandings of the distinction between biblically based monotheism and cosmological religions, its greater importance is in helping to explain a later historical process, one that is critical to understanding religion and culture today. This later process is referred to as *secularization,* and it will be considered in the following chapter.

Endnotes

1. See Karl Jaspers, *The Origin and Goal of History* (London: Routledge, 1953), 51ff.
2. The term *archaic* will be explicated a bit later in this chapter.
3. For a brief discussion of the concept of *mana* in the context of my usage here, and related concepts such as the Sioux *wakan,* the Iroquois *orenda,* the Huron *oki,* the West Indian *zemi,* and the Bambuti *megbe,* see Mircea Eliade, *Patterns in Comparative Religion* (New York: New American Library, 1963), 19–23.
4. Robert N. Bellah, *Beyond Belief: Essays on Religion in a Post-Traditionalist World* (Berkeley: University of California Press, 1970), 29.
5. Ibid., 31.
6. The one possible exception here would be China, which seems to have maintained much more of its primal animism and ancestrism, despite the deification of the emperor and large-scale seasonal rituals in archaic times.
7. Using generally accepted dates for *Enuma Elish* and *Gilgamesh.*
8. Bellah, 31.
9. See Peter Berger, *The Sacred Canopy: Elements of a Sociological Theory of Religion* (Garden City, NY: Anchor Books, 1969), 113–121.
10. For example, see Genesis 1:26–28 and 9:1–7 (NAB).

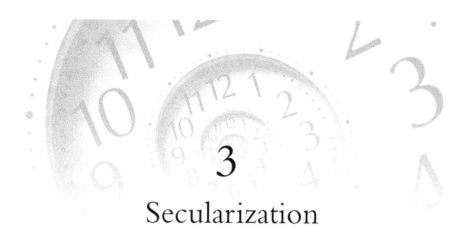

3

Secularization

Although the earliest manifestations of the principle of disenchantment were clearly religious in character, occurring in the process by which one type of religion desacralized the worldview of another, the principle of disenchantment is not restricted to cultural interactions between religions. In fact, it is often used to account for the process through which religious worldviews are desacralized by nonreligious processes and institutions. It is in this latter usage that the principle of disenchantment relates to secularization, a major theoretic concept and general thesis that offers an explanatory account of the role and status of religion in the modern West.

The concept of secularization is in flux today, and it is not the intent of this book to enter too far into the energetic dispute about its meaning, value, descriptive adequacy, and theoretic range. There is a rather massive body of literature on this topic, with the greatest number of texts coming out of sociology but including virtually all other fields in the social sciences and humanities. So vast is the literature on secularization and so diverse (and hotly contested) are positions on the topic that a primer such as this can only offer the broadest of overviews. This being the case, this chapter will offer a brief presentation of the "standard account" of the secularization thesis and the beginning of the next chapter will review major positions on the thesis, with note of representative thinkers and their texts.

The first section of this chapter will introduce the standard account in terms of the fundamental claims and key concepts of the thesis. The remainder of the chapter will summarize the standard account of the historical process of secularization in Western culture from its roots in the Christian worldview through the modern period.[1]

The historical summary will follow the standard account without apology, granting, of course, that this very account is being questioned and debated today. Also without apology, this primer recognizes the standard account as a necessary starting point for inquiries into religion and culture in the modern West. Whether the secularization thesis is accepted or rejected, its interpretation of history is valuable in and of itself; moreover, it is arguably one of the foundational interpretations of religion and culture in the modern West. Although this study takes quite seriously the various critiques of the thesis, it also recognizes that a solid grasp of the critiques requires familiarity with the thesis itself.

Finally, despite the necessity and value of the secularization thesis to understanding religion and culture in the modern West, it is also suggested here that, in its standard form, it perhaps serves better as a preface to inquiries into religion and culture in the contemporary (postmodern) world than as an adequate account in and of itself. In short, it is presumed here that a basic grasp of secularization is needed for an informed understanding of religion and culture in the modern West and as a starting point for inquiries into their relationship in the contemporary world.

The Secularization Thesis:
An Overview

Before examining the process of secularization, we must first equip ourselves with a working understanding of the secularization thesis, differing positions on the thesis, and the major thinkers who have contributed to its development (both constructively and "deconstructively"). For those interested in learning more about the thesis itself, its history, and its current status, there are several helpful texts. Two of particular note are "Secularization Theory: The Course of a Concept," by William H. Swatos, Jr., and Kevin J. Christiano, and Chapters 3 and 4 of *The Sociology of Religion*, by Grace Davie.[2] The first three chapters of Steve Bruce's *Religion in the Modern World* also give a good sketch of the main features of the thesis, although, unlike the generally neutral treatments of secularization in the other texts cited here, Bruce's work "is a robust defense of the body of ideas commonly designated the 'secularization thesis.' "[3] Perhaps the single most important thinker in the emergence, development, and (recent) reconsideration of secularization is Peter Berger, with his *The Sacred Canopy*[4] standing as the preeminent formulation of the standard account of secularization and its historical context. In this work, Berger builds on and synthesizes the work of earlier "classical sociologists," most notably Emile Durkheim, Karl Marx, and Max Weber, but his exposition of the theory and process of secularization is uniquely his own.

What, then, is meant by secularization in the context of the thesis with which it is associated? As with religion, the term is often defined, debated, and disputed. In brief, secularization is the process through which religion is marginalized within a society and its institutional position eclipsed by other institutions. Obviously, as this definition suggests, secularization presumes an earlier cultural situation when religion was more prominent in society and other institutions were less significant by comparison. In the West, this was medieval European culture, often referred to as *Christendom*—that is, Europe, as a unified culture system grounded in the Catholic religion. Less obvious, perhaps, but equally important to the thesis, is the presumption that with the rise of secularization there are various institutions that move to the position of cultural significance previously held by religion. Among these institutions, those typically cited include government, politics, economics, and science.

Expanding on this definition, Berger explains secularization as "the process by which sectors of society and culture are removed from the domination of religious institutions and symbols."[5] Importantly, he goes on to say that it manifests itself in both the material and intellectual realms. The material impact is the more obvious, being revealed in prohibitions on religious activity in government and public education (separation of church and state), and more radically in the expropriation of religious property and prohibitions of religious practices. The intellectual impact is even more significant, for in this way, secularization influences culture as a whole, affecting the arts, philosophy, literature, economics, and human self-understanding. Perhaps the most significant consequences of secularization's modification of culture is witnessed in the rise of science as an autonomous power in the modern world, the practical application of science in the technological revolution, and the economic application of technology in the Industrial Revolution.

Secularization, then, is a process, not an institution; and it is precisely that social and cultural process that relegates traditional religious affirmations, values, and institutions to secondary status at best, and in some instances (such as communist states) little or no status at all. What secularization does is loosen the grip of religion on society and the whole of culture in a general sense, and individual consciousness in myriad specific instances. In this account, religion does not disappear from the cultural scene, but its importance to individuals and culture as a whole declines.

It must be understood that in the standard account, secularization, per se, is neutral. In itself, it is a descriptive term; and as a general thesis (or collection of variations on a general thesis), it offers an explanation for a cultural process—namely, the marginalization of religion in modern Western culture. Notably, the standard account of secularization readily grants the continuance of religion in the face of (and often in opposition to) the secularization process.

As a descriptive term and general thesis, secularization has no agenda and no stake in any particular outcome. It is not a political ideology. Secularization does not seek to destroy religion, marginalize it, or separate it from the rest of culture. Individuals and social movements may well celebrate such goals and pursue them through various means, but those individuals and social movements are not following a doctrine in any way articulated by the secularization thesis. Perhaps they might be referred to as secularists or proponents of "secularism." In this regard, the beliefs and actions of an avowed secularist would be accounted for within the secularization thesis; then, again, however, so too would the beliefs and actions of an avowed religionist, who might be committed to strenuously resisting the process of secularization or the ideology of secularism. In itself, however, secularization is not an "ism"; it is a thesis that contains a descriptive component. One can debate the thesis (pro and con) and one can dispute its descriptive power and range; and, as we will see a bit later, there are certainly no limits to the debates and disputes spawned by the thesis.

Typically, secularization, or at least its emergence, is presented in the context of modernity, with the modern period (however it might be dated) representing a decisive break with the medieval period.[6] In this regard, secularization offers a theoretic explanation for the diminished role of religion in modern Western culture compared to its dominant role in the Middle Ages. As will be considered a bit later in this chapter, a number of historical events and various cultural processes initiated secularization and later supported and nourished its growth. Chief among these are the Protestant Reformation and, shortly thereafter (as Max Weber first observed), the rise of the capitalist economic system.[7]

Although many other elements could be included in an outline of the secularization thesis, those offered here are generally consistent in the standard account. The additional elements at times engender disagreements, but they are not the major point of dispute. The major point is whether the thesis is itself adequate. For working purposes, it will be presumed here that the account is valuable to understanding the relationship of religion and culture in the modern West.

***

As a process, secularization offers an explanation for both the emergence of the modern worldview in the period of the Renaissance and Reformation, as well as the expansion and maintenance of that worldview from that time up to our own. It explains how institutional energies and cultural forces that awakened in the Renaissance and Reformation loosened the grip first of medieval Catholicism and later of Christianity itself (Catholic and Protestant) on the societies and minds of Western Europe. Before isolating the forces that triggered the decisive eruption of secularization in the sixteenth and seventeenth centuries, a word must be said about its cultural context, and to do so, we must return to an earlier time, when the monotheistic impulse to desacralize and disenchant the world was interrupted by the rise of Christianity.

The Rise of Christianity and the Resacralization of the World

As noted in the previous chapter, the disenchantment of the world, so critical to the emergence of secularization, is traced to the Axial Age, and the initial expression of transcendental monotheism in the scriptures of Judaism. Also, as noted in that chapter, although ancient Judaism included the principle of disenchantment in its myths and worldview, it did not implement the principle to any historically significant extent. That was left to the later monotheisms— Christianity and Islam. Disenchantment as it transpires in the context of Islam is worthy of study; however, this book is focused on Christianity and the West, so it will have to suffice to observe that the course of the disenchantment process in Islam follows a distinctly different path from that followed by Christianity.

In fact, the disenchantment process in Christianity was not thoroughly initiated until the onset of the Reformation in the sixteenth century. Further, Christianity, in all of its forms, remains the most cosmological of the three monotheisms. This is due to the foundational belief in Christianity that the ultimate power (God) is incarnated in the person of Jesus. In short, divinity takes human form, thus mitigating the element of radical transcendence that is at the heart of the disenchantment process. This belief separates Christianity from both Judaism and Islam, and positions Christianity closer to those cosmological systems in which deities incarnate.

This basic theological affinity with cosmological religions did not, however, result in Christianity's acceptance of these religions. In fact, from its earliest cultural embodiments, Christianity vehemently rejected traditional cosmological religions—especially the polytheistic religions it encountered in the Roman Empire during its rise to power. As with Judaism, in its initial form, Christianity's rejection of cosmological systems was rhetorical and mythic; although countless Christians gave their lives due to this rejection.

The rise of Christianity to a position of religious dominance in the Roman Empire is much too detailed and complex to be more than summarized here. First, it can be noted that the development of Christianity from a small, apocalyptic Jewish sect into the official religion of the Roman Empire was incredibly rapid. Soon after the time of Jesus, Christianity began missionizing the Mediterranean world. Paul's work was vital, but the essential message of the religion had a powerfully attractive appeal to citizens of the empire. At its core were several key principles. First, the transcendental vision of a supernatural God and a supernatural concept of the human appealed to persons familiar with Hellenistic Judaism and the more mystical philosophic schools. Additionally, and in distinction to the capricious deities of Greco-Roman pantheon, this God cared for the fate of humanity and individuals, and gave instructions for living justly and righteously. Joined with this was a variation on cosmological belief; the incarnation of this God in human form and the sacrifice of this incarnation for the sake of his human followers. It was this sacrifice that would allow his followers the opportunity to dwell in paradise and, soon enough, to witness the radical transformation of the earth itself into a perfect world. This was not a pure transcendental monotheism, but rather, something of a hybrid of transcendental and cosmological beliefs. At the time of its emergence, it was one of many such hybrids in Roman culture.

In opposition to the young religion were two major forces: (1) the Roman government (and its state religion) and (2) other dynamic and attractive religions. A number of developments and innate features within the religion stand out as major factors contributing to the success of the movement in this period.

In response to challenges from the state, the religion relied on its universal appeal, fanatic support, and its growing acceptance by the upper classes. By the second century (100–200), the Roman army contained many Christians, thus making persecutions more difficult. Martyrs were excellent propaganda for the religion, as their fanatic support (even to death) helped convince others that there was something quite powerful about the faith they followed. Finally, the support of politically and economically advantaged classes tended to protect the religion and give it credence.

In response to the challenge posed by other religions and religious movements within Christianity, what became the Catholic Church began a process of institutionalization. The process resulted in official scriptures of the religion, established creeds outlining basic teachings, and a sanctioned clergy that conducted official rituals. The religion was further strengthened in its struggle with other faiths due to its universality, urban concentration, and (again) upper-class support.

By successfully overcoming both challenges, Christianity emerged as the only official religion of the Empire. In 313, Constantine issued the Edict of Milan giving Christianity legal status as a religion and in 380, the emperor Theodosius issued his famous decree, making Christianity the *only* legal religion in the empire (although Judaism was given a special exception).

During this period, the leaders of the Church met together on several occasions. These meetings were called General Councils, and the most notable ones were held at Nicea (325), Constantinople (381), and Chalcedon (451). These councils were convened to resolve issues and questions regarding Church teachings and organization.

The leaders of the Church during this period were dynamic, powerful, and interesting figures. They were genuine revolutionaries. They were also thinkers who had been schooled in Greek philosophy (especially the philosophy of the great idealist, Plato). Many were also outstanding speakers whose sermons would hold listeners spellbound for hours. In addition to their academic prowess and rhetorical aptitude, these men were also excellent organizers and managers. Most were politically literate, and many had experience in government and law. In short, these were talented individuals who knew "how things worked."

Augustine, Christendom, and Christianity's "Retrogressive Step"

Towering above all other thinkers of the early period was a bishop and theologian from North Africa, Augustine of Hippo (354-430). Arguably, the most influential thinker in the history of Christianity, and certainly in Western Christianity, Augustine inspired the religion's beliefs about original sin, just war, predestination, and the distinction between religion and secular culture. His legacy was not limited to Catholicism, as Protestantism embraced his teachings as well. Without the theology of Augustine, Christianity and the culture it dominated would have a very different appearance today.

Among Augustine's numerous works, two are of enormous importance to the culture of the West: *Confessions* and *The City of God*. The former was an autobiography, a theology of the individual that narrated how a sophisticated Roman citizen came to embrace the new religion of Christianity. The latter offered a theology of culture that interpreted human history as the interaction between two contrasting institutions or worldviews—the Earthly City and the City of God. The Earthly City was unstable, prone to disruption, the rise and fall of nations, informed by the pursuit of material power and success, and populated by persons destined for divine punishment. The City of God, on the other hand, was non-material, oblivious to the vicissitudes of the Earthly City, represented (but not manifested) by the Church, and populated by individuals seeking God above all else. As *Confessions* offered emerging Christian culture a model for individual religious life, *The City of God* presented a template for Western culture itself, one that drew a clear bright line between the religious realm and the rest of human life. That the non-religious realm was relegated to an inferior status supported religious domination of society, but it also lead to unintended consequences—most notably, creation of the cultural foundation for secularization in its sharp contrast between the religious realm of culture (the City of God) and the non-religious realm (the Earthly City).

Long before the rise of secularization, however, *The City of God* offered a blueprint for a culture in which Christianity served as the source of sacred legitimation. This culture emerged in the 5th century as the social and political order of the Roman Empire began to disintegrate. By this time, Christianity had spread beyond the Mediterranean Basin and the confines of the empire, unifying Europe religiously, but not politically; and creating *Christendom*, a cultural system that would last for a thousand years.

With the rise of Christendom, Christianity moved, somewhat unevenly but certainly relentlessly, to eliminate the indigenous cosmological religions of Europe. This was facilitated through missionary activities and with the support of the new governing entities that replaced the old Roman Empire with a wide array of small states. Concurrent with its expansion and consolidation of cultural power, Christianity underwent a notable transformation. Berger describes it as a "retrogressive step in terms of the secularizing motifs of the Old Testament."[8] What he means, in terms of the concepts developed here, is that Christianity assumed cosmological features. In many instances these features were appropriated rather directly from the indigenous cosmological religions Christianity encountered and in others they were unique modifications predicated on cosmological tendencies present in Christianity itself. In fact, it could be argued that at least after its legalization in the fourth century (if not for some time before), Christianity was essentially a cosmological religion; and only with the Reformation did it take on more traditional transcendental features.

Besides the incarnation, previously mentioned, the inventory of significant cosmological features includes the trinitarian concept of deity, the nature and function of saints, the ritual of transubstantiation, the sacralization of unique geographic locales as pilgrimage sites, the veneration of relics, and the reaffirmation of priestly administration of rituals. The liturgical year, itself essentially cosmological in character, designated holy days using those previously sacralized by cosmological religions, including Easter, Christmas, and All Saints' Day. In short, Christianity—as it came to exist as the ultimate source for the legitimation of the medieval social order—was hardly a classical transcendental religion. Arguably, it had more in common with archaic cosmological religions than the transcendental monotheism affirmed in Judaism. On the eve of the sixteenth century, it also had no serious opposition. Culturally, it was the only sacred game in town. The game was about to change, however, and so was the town.

The Eruption of Secularization

The secularization process proper is correctly traced to the Renaissance-Reformation period, perhaps more specifically, the fifteenth and sixteenth centuries. Although the groundwork was prepared by ancient transcendental religious notions, and most directly by Augustine's theology of culture, secularization in the modern period was an entirely novel and radiant force.

To understand the modern secularization process, we might best proceed much as we did in our approach to the disenchantment process initiated by the biblical worldview. That is, by comparison of the new worldview with the resident one that it challenged and rather swiftly delegitimized. In the case of modern secularization, the worldview that it challenged and soon replaced was that of medieval Catholicism—a religion with certain salient features reminiscent of the cosmological religions of antiquity.

In surveying late-medieval Catholicism, we are at once struck by its affinities with cosmological religions. Although the triumph of the Catholic form of Christianity over the polytheism of the Roman Empire seemed at first glance to be a victory of the transcendental religious vision over the cosmological, as we have noted, the triumph was paradoxical, for with the rise of Catholicism came a host of cosmological elements, and at the very least a process of re-cosmicization. Perhaps it was no transcendental triumph at all, but only a transition from one type of cosmological system to another. However it may be conceived, the unified religious base of late-medieval European culture was shattered by the Protestant Reformation.

It was to medieval Catholicism that Luther, Calvin, and other reformers were reacting; and in effect, the Reformation replicated in Western Europe the disenchantment process of antiquity. As had been the case in that earlier time, a thoroughly mediated and unified religious worldview was challenged on the basis of a radically transcendental understanding of divinity. Berger captures the full seriousness and extent of the situation:

> The Protestant believer no longer lives in a world ongoingly penetrated by sacred beings and forces. Reality is polarized between a radically transcendent divinity and a radically fallen humanity. . . . Between them lies an altogether "natural" universe. . . . The radical transcendence of God confronts a universe of radical immanence, of "closedness" to the sacred. . . . Protestantism abolished most . . . mediations. It broke the continuity, cut the umbilical cord between heaven and earth, and thereby threw man back upon himself in a historically unprecedented manner.[9]

This is the Protestant version of disenchantment. In principle, it is no different from the disenchantment process articulated in the scriptures of Judaism. In fact, it is a reaffirmation of that principle in the context of Christianity—a reaffirmation that had not occurred in the religion's first millennium. What is different, however, between the Protestant version of disenchantment and the version witnessed in early Judaism, is that Protestantism quickly became a powerful political and economic force.

What Protestantism also did, especially in Luther's modification of Augustine's concept of the "two cities" (the City of God and the Earthly City), was grant religious sanction to the human city—and with it, secular culture. No longer was secular culture (the human city) relegated to secondary status beside the Church (which represented the City of God). Secular culture became a place in which God could be served just as fully as the Church. Calvin would take this religious validation of secular activity even further by equating the concept of divine election with material well-being and economic success.

By validating the secular world, Protestantism also devalued the world of religious meaning. In one sense this was a cunning theological tactic, for by challenging the Catholic assumption that life's ultimate meaning could be found only through the Church, the Protestant impulse to legitimate the secular world served to delegitimate the Catholic religion. In a more profound sense, it was a colossal blunder, since the recognition of the viability of a secular society was a de facto recognition of the autonomy of secular society apart from any religious affirmation, Catholic or Protestant. To combat Catholic claims of religious ultimacy, Protestantism aligned itself with forces outside the religious sphere. In the case of Luther, the alliance was with the forces of nationalism in Germany; in the case of Calvin, it was with the forces of emerging capitalism. In both cases, the alliance was efficacious to the cause of the new religion. The alliance between Protestantism and the emerging forces of secularization, however, turned out to be a Faustian bargain, for ultimately, secularization would delegitimate all religious claims to ultimacy, which is to say, it would delegitimate religion itself. Ironically, due to the Reformation, what was previously deemed secular now assumed the role of the sacred.

The Protestant attack on Catholicism can be seen as the spark that triggered the modern secularization process, and while that attack has certain similarities with early Judaism's challenge to cosmological worldviews, there is an important distinction. What makes the situation of the Reformation different from the ancient situation is that in the Reformation the legitimacy of a non-religious (secular) world was affirmed by religion itself. Rather than depreciated, it was now, in the view of the Protestants, *the arena of God's glory*. Initially, this legitimacy was tacit and perhaps only expedient; but over time, this legitimacy increased until, by the Enlightenment, the secular world had the power to assert not only its full autonomy from religion, but also its greater legitimacy than religion. Unlike the ancient struggle, the encounter here was not between two rival religions, but rather between religion and an irreligious worldview—at least that is how the struggle has been interpreted traditionally.

Citing the Reformation as the spark of the secularization process is only the beginning of the story. The process itself extends well beyond the Reformation and, in fact, according to some, up to the present day. As they argue, between then and now the process has continued unchecked, but it has been punctuated by several significant events and driven by several historical forces.

The first event of note actually occurred before the Reformation, in 1454. In that year Johann Gensfleisch of Gutenberg perfected movable type and the printing press was born. It has been argued that Luther's "95 Theses" of 1517 would never have touched off the Reformation had it not been for the printing press. Equally arguable is the decisiveness of the press to the secularization process. What the press did was nothing short of a transformation of society. Suddenly, the amount of knowledge to which people had access was tremendously expanded. Before this invention, very few books could be produced, and, as a corollary, very few people could read and very few had the opportunity to study and learn. Before the press, few knew the events of the past—what Rome was, what history was all about. Before Gensfleisch's breakthrough, few knew geography—the location of nations and peoples, rivers and oceans. Before the press, few knew mathematics of even the simplest sort. Whatever the average person knew was probably received from the Church, and the Church as an institution was less than democratic in its educational mission and very resistant to change. Once the press came into existence, however, change was inevitable, and the Church could go along or be left behind. That it was left behind is part of the secularization process.

The next decisive event was the Thirty Years' War and the Peace of Westphalia in 1648. As a result of this war, which was fought largely on the basis of religious differences, the importance of religion was drastically reduced and its practice became largely a private rather than a public concern. For over a thousand years, the central feature of cultural life and individual existence had been the Church. Beginning with the Renaissance and the Protestant Reformation, and fueled by over a century of religious violence (of which the Thirty Years' War was the culmination), Christianity began to lose its hold on the minds and hearts of Western Europeans. Just as after the Peace of Westphalia, religion was not something worth killing or being killed for, so too did it cease to be a driving force in cultural life. This is another part of the secularization process.

In the wake of the Thirty Years' War and with the erosion of religion as a motivating force in cultural life, new institutions of a decidedly secular character arose. Some of the major new institutions that vied for the interest and devotion of the masses were education, politics, nationalism, and economics. In the case of each of these institutions, persons were given opportunities for self-identification apart from religion. In each case, persons who once would have identified themselves in religious terms and looked to the Church to explain their role in society, could now look elsewhere for self-legitimation. As a consequence, religion was devalued in society and its sphere of cultural influence drastically contracted. Thus, while I might be a Christian, I was first what I was educated to be, perhaps a lawyer, or a scientist, an engineer, a teacher. If I were a politician or involved in political issues, I might still be a Christian, but I was first a Democrat, a Monarchist, or, later, a Socialist or a Marxist. If I were a nationalist, I might still be a Christian, but I was first a Frenchman, a Pole, an Englishman, a German, a Serb. In economic terms, I might still be a Christian, but I was first a capitalist, a merchant, a tenant, an investor, a landlord, an employee. The great change, and the turn toward secularization revealed by the development of these new institutions for self-definition, is that until this time, the vast majority of Europeans did not identify themselves apart from religion and religious categories of existence. Additionally, most were uneducated agriculturalists with few, if any, material possessions and no property, usually ruled on one hand by a powerful lord and on the other by an even more powerful Church.

The Enlightenment and the First Flowering of Secularization

Beyond the crucible of the Renaissance and the Reformation, the next great era of consequence in the standard account of the secularization process was the Enlightenment. It was at this time that secularization became fully established as the secular vision forcefully asserted its dominance over society and religion. Whether the Enlightenment is over or not is a debatable point, but even if the Enlightenment is simply an historical era (i.e., the eighteenth and nineteenth centuries), it is an era whose chief themes and forces continue to powerfully influence the West.

The origin of the word tells us much about the ideology of the Enlightenment: "The Enlightenment" *(Aufklärung)* was first used by eighteenth century thinkers to characterize their times over and against the medieval period, which, in contrast, came to be known as the *Dark Ages*. In its most forceful denotation, the term expressed an anti-religious stance, since the "darkness" of medievalism (against which the "light" of eighteenth century culture was contrasted) was a darkness caused by superstition and ignorance attributed to the religious domination of society. In its social and cultural vision, the Enlightenment stressed secular non-religious knowledge and, just as the social, political, and academic leaders of ancient Rome left their polytheistic religions for the new religion of Christianity during the Christian revolution of the second through fourth centuries, so the leaders of eighteenth century Europe left the Christian religion for the various movements in the orbit of secularization.

During the Enlightenment, science bloomed, the horizons of intellectual inquiry expanded, and everything was questioned and doubted until proven true according to the emerging materialist ethic of the time. New inventions and technologies proliferated, and they continued to change the world, just as the printing press had done at the beginning of the secularization process. Concurrent with the Enlightenment were three revolutions: the American Revolution, the French Revolution, and the Industrial Revolution—each representing important motifs of modernization. The American Revolution, initiated in 1776, features a large-scale commitment to violence (a war) predicated on secular ideals: economic freedom, political self-determination, and nationalism. This was not a revolution predicated on religious beliefs, and in its wake came a host of societal structures typical of secularization: the institutionalization and legalization of the separation of the religious and secular realms, the beginning of state-supported pluralism, and, in the name of religious freedom, the free and open competition between religions for the allegiance of believers.

The French Revolution, sparked in 1789, also reveals features common to many other modern political revolutions. Again, violence was legitimated on the basis of secular ideals—liberty, equality, fraternity. The brutality of the revolutionaries was alarming and legendary, and in this instance, religion itself was attacked. Along with the French aristocracy, the revolutionaries targeted the Catholic Church. Church properties were nationalized, clerics were forced to vow allegiance to the state, and statues symbolizing secular ideals (e.g., Reason and Liberty) were erected in church buildings. Even more than the American Revolution, the French Revolution represented the aggressive assertion of a secular worldview, and the destructive potential of this worldview to religion. Finally, in place of a king, who ruled by divine right, an authoritarian leader (Napoleon) took control of the state and commenced military action against the rest of Europe in an attempt to establish an empire. Subsequent secular revolutions have followed a similar path.

Finally, with the Industrial Revolution, came the expansion and complexification of manufacturing, intensified urbanization, and the stratification of society along economic lines. The result was an unprecedented transformation of Western culture; one to which religion was ill prepared to respond or even fully understand.

A popular date given for the beginning of the Industrial Revolution is 1769. In that year, James Watt (a Scottish engineer) perfected the first efficient steam engine. It is of note that only five years later, Watt joined with Matthew Boulton to establish a company to manufacture the engines.[10] This little footnote to the invention of the steam engine tells us much about how the Industrial Revolution worked and continues to work to this day.

It is not just a new invention or the perfection of a new technology that changes the world. What changed the world is not what James Watt did, but what he and Matthew Boulton did. What changed transportation was not the invention of the car; what changed transportation and, with it, all of American society, was Henry Ford's assembly line. The cultural logic of an industrialized culture is not based on the discovery of new devices but on the discovery of ways to reproduce and distribute the devices on a massive scale.

This is what the Industrial Revolution tells us, and we have to really take a step back behind Watt's steam engine to find what may actually be the event that triggered this revolution. Rather than Watt's engine of 1769, this event may well be the perfection of a manufacturing device by John Kay in 1733.

Kay's machine was called the flying shuttle, and it allowed weavers to produce cloth more rapidly and in greater widths than had ever been possible before. Thirty years later (1764), James Hargreaves perfected a machine, called the "spinning jenny" (named after his wife or daughter), that could spin eight threads of yarn simultaneously. Hargreaves' jennys thus augmented the productive capacity of Kay's shuttles by greatly increasing the quantity of thread available for their use. Then, by the early 1770s, the productive capacity of both (and their successor machines) was increased geometrically by the proliferation of steam engines. In 1789, the first steam-powered cotton factory was built in Manchester, England; and "by the early 1800s nearly all spinning and weaving was being done in factories, after having been a home process for thousands of years."[11]

What these inventions allowed was an incredible increase in the production of textiles—fabrics. With the increase in fabrics came an increase in clothing and a reduction in costs for apparel. Soon enough raw materials (wool and cotton) began to be consumed at incredible rates. Cotton became the preferred material, because wool production could not keep up with the demand. A direct consequence of this was a dramatic increase in the cultivation of cotton, chiefly in the southern part of the United States, and with this came a corresponding increase in the use of human slaves as agricultural workers.

The flying shuttle was, of course, just the beginning, and this, too, is what makes the birth of industrialization so revolutionary, and so critical to the emergence of the modern West. There had been other remarkable discoveries and inventions in the past, to be sure (metallurgy, the compass, gun powder, the printing press, optical devices, the wheel), but what happened beginning in the late eighteenth century had never happened before.

First, the new devices and manufacturing processes proliferated at an astonishing rate. Second, the new devices tended to be synergistically related, as one new device often led to the invention of others of direct benefit to the first (as with the jenny and the shuttle). Third, each new manufacturing technology was quickly standardized and then replicated over and over again. The steam-powered factory in Manchester in 1789, previously noted, after all, was only the *first*. Other factories would follow. Fourth, the new inventions tended to be focused on the mass production of material goods (commodities). The end result was the rise of a culture based on an economic system driven by vast numbers of factories producing an ever-expanding stream of commodities—textiles, bullets, clothing, nails, shoes, circular saws, cotton gins, and so on. Fifth, needless to say, and as is well-known today, with the rise of industrial culture, there was a correspondingly swift degradation of the natural environment. The ecological consequences of the Industrial Revolution were devastating—and they continue to be.

Writing of the impact of the Industrial Revolution, Marx observed:

> Constant revolutionizing of production, uninterrupted uncertainty and agitation distinguish [this] epoch from all earlier ones. All fixed, fast-frozen relations, with their train of ancient and venerable prejudices and opinions are swept away, all new-formed ones become antiqued before they can ossify. All that is solid melts into air, all that is holy is profaned, and man is at last compelled to face his real conditions of life, and his mutual relations with a sober eye.[12]

Among those venerable prejudices and opinions being swept away were those long safeguarded by religion. The Industrial Revolution transformed the West with stunning celerity. Not only was the natural environment ravished, so too was the social environment. Families were dislocated, traditional communities were wrecked, and the pulse of life accelerated. Religion, which was already shaken by the wars of religion and the wrenching dismemberment of Christendom, was staggered again as its concept of the world was stunningly disenchanted. In the place of the world legitimated by Christian myths and rituals dating back to antiquity, the West discovered a new world, one with myths and rituals befitting an industrial culture: myths of technology and mass production, and rituals of factory labor and production quotas. Where the cultural centers of medieval life had been churches, the cultural centers of modern industrial life were factories—Blake's "dark Satanic mills."

***

Besides the revolutions that transformed the political and economic landscape of the West, the Enlightenment also brought a far-reaching intellectual revolution. Like the others, it has had a long-lasting negative impact on religion. This primer is not the place to go into extensive detail about the many thinkers of the Enlightenment who critiqued religion and its claims. Still, some must be mentioned, for they exemplify the process through which the intellectual community directly attacked the plausibility structures of religion. Each of these thinkers, and the intellectual milieu as a whole, dealt religion a devastating blow by attacking it at its very core—certainty and finality. In an age of assertive inquiry, religious claims of certainty and finality seemed empty and meaningless for all but the "unenlightened."

To set the strategy, although not necessarily the main religious theme for the intellectual revolution of the Enlightenment, we can look at the work of René Descartes. It was Descartes who introduced systematic doubt as a working philosophic methodology. Of course, Descartes is best remembered for the *"Cogito,"* but his real importance to the Enlightenment and the entire intellectual ambiance of modernity is his preface to *"Cogito ergo sum"* (I think therefore I am); namely, the *"Dubito"*: *"Dubito ergo cogito"* (I doubt, therefore I think). For Descartes, all things could be doubted, except, initially, the fact that he doubted. The importance of this approach is that Descartes predicated his philosophic inquiry not on received truths or faith, but, rather, on doubt. If he had not doubted, he would never have concluded that he thought. Doubt, then, was the key to the Cartesian system, and was a critical element in the foundation of modern intellectual history. Descartes did go on to construct arguments for God's existence that were not unlike those of medieval theologians before him, Anselm and Aquinas. Those arguments, however, did not set the tone for modern thought. What set the tone was the doubt, and the thinkers of the Enlightenment picked up where Descartes left off and moved on to test the limits of human knowing and meaning.

The Western intellectual tradition has followed Descartes' strategy in one way or another ever since. In the wake of Descartes came Hume, Kant, Hegel, Kierkegaard, Nietzsche, and Marx. Each of these figures found religion as it had existed before the Enlightenment somehow unfulfilled and inauthentic. Each tampered with traditional Christian assumptions, and Hume, Kierkegaard, Nietzsche, and Marx blasted institutional Christianity from pillar to post. Each contributed to the secular-modernist understanding of religion, and each informed the intellectuals of the West that there is something decisively wrong with religion in theory or practice or both. Most emblematic of the secular-modernist stance toward religion is perhaps this passage from Nietzsche:

> The madman jumped into their midst and pierced them with his eyes. "Whither is God?" he cried; "I will tell you. *We have killed him*—you and I. All of us are his murderers. . . . God is dead. God remains dead. And we have killed him."[13]

What started with Descartes' doubt of all things and moved to his philosophic proof for the existence of God, led to Nietzsche's philosophic rejection of religion and his affirmation that God is dead. Although rather dramatic in its phrasing, Nietzsche's position is not significantly different from the standard account of the secularization thesis. In fact, a leading proponent of the thesis, Steve Bruce, uses the affirmation, "God is dead," as the title of one of his more important books.[14] Dramatic rhetoric aside, Bruce is in essential agreement with Nietzsche. For all intents and purposes, religion has been rejected as the primary source of meaning and value for Western culture, and the God of Christianity is functionally deceased—or so the standard account would have it.

Whether this account is still valid, however, is the subject of vigorous dispute today. The context and contours of this dispute will be considered in the next chapter.

Endnotes

1. The modern period denoted here dates from the middle of the seventeenth century (and specifically, the end of the Thirty Years' War [1648]) to the advent of the contemporary (postmodern) period, which will here be cited with a marker date of 1950. Additional details on this method of periodization will be given in Chapter 4.

2. See William H. Swatos, Jr., and Kevin J. Christiano, "Secularization Theory: The Course of a Concept," in *The Secularization Debate,* ed. Swatos and Daniel V. A. Olson (Lanham, MD, Rowman and Littlefield, 2000), 1–20; and Grace Davie, *The Sociology of Religion* (Los Angeles: Sage, 2007), chaps. 3 and 4 (46–88). Chapter 4 of Davie's book focuses on *rational choice theory,* which, in its application to religion, stands as the most notable basis for contra-secularization arguments.

3. Steve Bruce, *Religion in the Modern World: From Cathedrals to Cults* (Oxford: Oxford University Press, 1996), chaps. 1–3 (1–68). Quotation in text, 6.

4. Peter Berger, *The Sacred Canopy* (Garden City, NY: Anchor Books, 1969).

5. Ibid., 107. This is Berger's "simple definition of secularization . . ."

6. See note 1.

7. Weber recognizes a nexus between the Protestant Reformation and the rise of the capitalist economic system in his famous work on the subject. See Max Weber, *The Protestant Ethic and the Spirit of Capitalism,* trans. Talcott Parsons (New York: Scribner's, 1958).

8. Berger, 121.

9. Ibid., 111–112.

10. Jean Cooke, et al., *History's Timeline* (New York: Crescent Books, 1981), 162.

11. Ibid. Necessary to add, it was also an *artisan process* for much of human history.

12. Karl Marx and Friedrich Engels, *The Communist Manifesto,* trans. Samuel Moore (New York: Washington Square Press, 1964), 63.

13. Friedrich Nietzsche, *The Gay Science,* trans. Walter Kaufmann (New York: Vintage Books, 1974), 181.

14. See Steve Bruce, *God is Dead: Secularization in the West* (Oxford: Blackwell, 2002).

4

The Secularization Dispute and Beyond: Religion and Western Culture Today

The Secularization Dispute Today

With apologies to William Swatos and Daniel Olson,[1] disagreements about secularization seem better characterized as a dispute than a debate. If it is a debate, it is an intense one, at least at times. It often seems more like a heated argument, one in which decorum is not always present and the positions of one's opponents are not treated with respect or even seriously engaged. Frankly, in many instances, the arena of dispute seems to resemble the rough and tumble world of politics, with attacks running back and forth from both sides and debates where candidates present mini-lectures that may have no relevance to specific questions posed by moderators or their fellow candidates. Why all the heat? Well, an oft-cited truism gets us near a good explanation: *When there is conflict there is something at stake.* The greater the conflict, the more is at stake. What is at stake in the secularization dispute is the role and function of religion in the contemporary world. Hence, the heat.

It is not the intent of this primer to enter into the dispute, although I do have a position on the topic.[2] It is also beyond the range of this primer to examine more than a few of the major positions in the dispute. However, the contours of this dispute must be borne in mind when studying religion in the contemporary West. Without this preliminary awareness, the authority of one or another text might be overestimated and the merits of alternative views underestimated or missed entirely. Suffice it to say, there is no authoritative position today, and few scholars endorse the thesis without qualification.

Although there are many nuances to be found in contemporary approaches to secularization, a clear distinction can be drawn between two major camps and two major periods. The first division separates those who reject the secularization thesis and those who, despite certain challenges, find that it has merit. The second division separates the period of ascendancy for the thesis (1960s to 1980s) from the period of its reconsideration (1990s to present).

Proponents

In the first period, a number of important works by influential thinkers helped establish secularization as the central theory for interpreting the status and function of religion in the modern world. The list of thinkers and works is quite extensive, but only a select number will be noted here. As previously noted, Peter Berger's *The Sacred Canopy* (1967)[3] is a leading source for the standard account of secularization and its historical context. Berger's many other works in the early period also focused on religion in the context of secularization. Of particular note are *The Homeless Mind* (1973) and *The Heretical Imperative* (1979).[4]

Equal in rank to Berger in the formative development of the theory is Bryan Wilson, whose notable early contributions include *Religion in Secular Society* (1969) and *Contemporary Transformations of Religion* (1976).[5] A later article by Wilson, "The Secularization Thesis: Criticisms and Rebuttals" (1998),[6] is also especially keen in its presentation of the thesis and defenses against its critics. Karel Dobbelaere's "Secularization: A Multi-Dimensional Concept" (1981)[7] is also among the important contributions to the development of the theory. An often over looked proponent is Political Scientist, Marcel Gauchet, who deployed the thesis with only slight modifications in *The Disenchantment of the World* (1997).[8] For Gauchet, transcendental elements Christianity inherited from Judaism, long mitigated in Catholicism, eventually reemerged in Protestantism, leading to Christianity's inability to legitimate culture, and its replacement by new (non-religious) sources of legitimation, particularly political institutions. Finally, a major theological interpretation of the secularization thesis was offered by Harvey Cox in his widely read book, *The Secular City* (1965).[9]

As is obvious from the title of Wilson's 1998 article, by the latter part of the twentieth century, the secularization thesis had critics—many of them, in fact. It also had supporters, including Wilson, Dobbelaere, and Gauchet—but, notably, not Berger. Foremost among its contemporary champions is Steve Bruce, who has defended the thesis against major challenges brought by critics. Bruce's position is best revealed in two representative works, *Religion in the Modern World: From Cathedrals to Cults* (1996) and *God Is Dead: Secularization in the West* (2002).[10] Each presents a summary of the standard account, rebuttals of criticisms, and selected case studies of religion in the contemporary West. The rebuttals of Bruce and Wilson are noteworthy in light of the following section, which summarizes the major criticisms of the secularization thesis. These criticisms are significant, but it must be remembered that they are not without rebuttals from defenders of the thesis.

Besides the proponents of the thesis, there are a number of important thinkers who take a more nuanced approach. Among the more notable are Yves Lambert, Grace Davis, Vincent Pecora, and Charles Taylor. Each maintains elements of the thesis but qualifies its reach.[11] Lambert recognizes two "thresholds of secularization" (decline in religious authority and elimination of religious symbolism) and claims that the first threshold has been passed, but not the second. Davie, for her part, offers the concept of "multiple modernities" and "conceptual maps," recognizing that there is diversity in the way different cultures undergo the modernization process and, hence, different maps (like the secularization thesis or rational choice theory) are required to help us navigate diverse cultural terrains. Pecora finds religion and secularization in a dialectical relationship, in which religion persists as a "semantic resonance" in the midst of secular culture. Contrasting himself with "traditional" secularization theorists, Taylor identifies three concepts of "secularity," which focus, respectively, on: society, individuals, and cultural consciousness. Favoring the third, he argues that even in such secular systems references to transcendental religiosity tend to reappear.

Critics

Perhaps the first notable critic of the secularization theory is David Martin, whose article, "Towards Eliminating the Concept of Secularization" (1965),[12] was a clear challenge to the developing acceptance of the theory. His objections were further developed in his subsequent works, including his major work, *A General Theory of Secularization* (1978); articles, such as "The Secularization Issue"; and, more recently, *On Secularization: Towards a Revised General Theory* (2005).[13] Martin's challenge, in brief, is that the theory is of greatest relevance to modern European culture and that it is less helpful in accounting for the status of religion in other cultures. Martin was also instrumental in developing a critique of the thesis on the basis of the claim that it presumed an earlier period of religious fervor (a golden age of faith) prior to the rise of secularization.

A more hostile critique was offered in 1986 by Jeffery Hadden. As explained by Swatos and Kevin Christiano:

> The core of his argument is that in and from its genesis secularization constituted a *"doctrine* more than a theory" based on "presuppositions that . . . represent a taken-for-granted *ideology."* . . . Over time in social scientific circles . . . *"the idea of secularization became sacralized."*[14]

In short, this type of challenge contends that secularization is an academic dogma rather than a genuine theory, and that scholars accept the thesis, not because it is well supported or gives an accurate account of religion, but because of pressures within the academy. Hadden, and others, conclude that religion is alive, well, and flourishing in the contemporary world.

One of the most recognized critics of the secularization thesis, Rodney Stark, certainly agrees with Hadden. Stark and various associates (notably William Bainbridge, Roger Finke, and Laurence Iannaccone) are arguably the leading opponents of the secularization thesis today. It is not just that they challenge the standard account of the secularization thesis (as, for example, Stark's "Secularization, R.I.P."[15]), they go considerably further, offering an alternative and contradictory theory that accounts for the vitality of religion in the contemporary world. This alternative is a variation of a general theory used in the social sciences known as *rational choice theory* (RCT). As nicely summarized by Davie, as it applies to religion, RCT is largely an American approach that "postulates that individuals are naturally religious (to be so is part of the human condition) and will activate their religious choices, just like any other choices, in order to maximize gain (however conceptualized) and to minimize loss."[16]

Unlike the secularization thesis, RCT thus recognizes religion as an elemental feature of cultural life, if not a fundamental human need, and its presence in society as a cultural necessity. It goes further to claim, as Stark and Bainbridge affirm in *The Future of Religion* (1985):

> Having erroneously equated religion with a particular set of religious organizations, Western intellectuals have misread the secularization of these groups as the doom of religion in general. But it is foolish to look only at sunsets and never observe the dawn: this history of religion is not only a pattern of decline; it is equally a portrait of birth and growth. We argue that the sources of religion are shifting constantly in societies but that *the amount of religion remains relatively constant.*[17]

To the degree that the secularization thesis seeks to minimize the significance of religion, it misinterprets the role of religion in human culture, according to Stark and Bainbridge. Moreover, should the thesis be construed to predict an eventual disappearance of religion, it is grievously wrong. Finally, if "the amount of religion remains constant" within a culture system, secularization is impossible—a point acknowledged and rebutted by Bruce, by the way, in his critique of Stark and Bainbridge.[18] Besides the texts already noted, other works countering the secularization thesis from the RCT community include Stark and Iannaccone's "A Supply-side Reinterpretation of the 'Secularization of Europe'" (1994) and Stark and Finke's *Acts of Faith* (2000).[19]

From among the many other criticisms of the secularization thesis that could be included here, none is more telling than that of Peter Berger, one of the first major proponents of the thesis. Berger today has had a major change of heart. The title of a recent book of essays, which he edited, expresses this change of heart most vividly: *The Desecularization of the World.*[20] In his introduction to the collection, Berger writes, quite candidly: "My point is that the assumption that we live in a secularized world is false. The world today, with some exceptions . . . is as furiously religious as it ever was."[21] He then proceeds to summarize what he perceives to be the various errors in the secularization thesis, especially as they are revealed in resurgence of religion in the contemporary world. The chapters that follow focus on the resurgence of religion in various parts of the world, with the obvious intent of supporting the contention contained in the title.

This chapter could continue on (perhaps interminably) citing additional sources of support for the theory, others in opposition, and others (perhaps the largest group) offering nuanced treatments. It is obvious, however, that the secularization thesis is disputed today, and there are hardened positions (pro and con) on its merits. Readers are left to their own interpretations—and they are certainly encouraged to review the literature on the subject, some of which has been presented here. It is the contention of this primer, however, that grasping the primary aspects of the secularization thesis (presented in Chapter 3) is necessary for understanding religion in modern Western culture and, initially at least, encountering religion in the contemporary West.

Modernity and Postmodernity

What, then, can be said about religion in contemporary culture? Among other reasonable assertions is that, for many, the status of religion is framed by an approach that characterizes contemporary culture as *postmodern*. The introduction of this term is not intended as a definitive classification of contemporary culture, nor does this primer aim to resolve the complex nest of issues commingled in and around the term *postmodern*. The term is in extreme flux today, in part due to its magnificent popularity in both popular and academic culture. Certainly not without its critics, it remains one of those alluring labels that at once classifies an incredibly vast array of cultural phenomena while simultaneously (and necessarily) defying any and all efforts to stabilize its meaning with anything close to precision. It is a term of conjure and conjecture, and ultimately, I suspect, uncertainty for many. This uncertainty may not be diminished here, although it is my hope to present the concept of postmodernity in an introductory manner without minimizing the genuine complexities associated with the ever-expanding dialogue about its meaning.

First, whatever else may be meant by postmodern, it is clearly intended to mark a cultural epoch following the modern period. Modernity has been presented previously in the context of secularization. To what was said previously, we can add that modernity is driven by industrialization, the disintegration of earlier social structures (such as feudalism, small-scale agrarian communities, and the religious organization of time), and the rise of new social structures (the nation-state, the corporation, and the monetization of time).

Some selected elements, institutions, ideals, and forces typically associated with modernity, include the following:

Replacement of a religious worldview by a scientific worldview

Celebration of science as a liberating force

The myth of perfectibility and perpetual advance through rational inquiry

"Novus ordo seclorum" (found on the reverse of the Great Seal of the United States)

Humanism

Capitalism and the emergence of industrial capitalism

The quest to understand, organize, and control society through rational means

Secularization

Democratization and the emergence of political parties

Positivism and the idealization of scientific method

The quest for universal truth(s) and "the spirit of discovery"

Bureaucratization

Compulsory education, universal literacy, and text-based communication

Euro-American colonialism

Heightened individualism

"The spirit of discovery"

Nationalism

The autonomy of human reason

The quest to subdue and master nature (including human nature)

Social compartmentalizations and dichotomies, such as private/public, church/state, labor/management, family/job)

Rise of the mass media and popular culture

Development of religious denominations

These cultural features and ideals help identify and distinguish modernity as the historical period following and replacing the medieval—both in terms of human consciousness and historical periods. Thus, the beginning of modernity is often traced to events, movements, and persons seen as marking the end of the medieval period, and, specifically, the end of religious domination of society, feudal economic systems, and scientific/technological inertia.

Dates for its emergence are wide-ranging. It could be traced to the Renaissance (1453/1454), the Reformation (1517), the life of René Descartes (1596–1650), or any of many other possible candidates. For working purposes, the end of the Thirty Years' War (1648) seems quite satisfactory, since it marked the end of the last great European war in which religion was a major inspiration. In short, after 1648 religion was not a compelling motivating force for personal and institutional violence. More bluntly, it was not worth dying for; and even more to the point, it was not worth killing for, or sending one's children forth to kill and die for.

The consideration of the power of religion (or any other dominant cultural institution) on the basis of one's willingness to die for it is derived, in part, from Roger Corless' treatment of a portion of Ninian Smart's *Beyond Ideology: Religion and the Future of Western Civilization,* and Corless' comments on "what-you-would-die-for-isms."[22] The Corless-Smart notion of *die-for-isms* is relevant to considerations of religion in the contemporary world, where we again see people willing to die for religion. I would only add that the distinct relevance of this notion is brought into even sharper clarity when the other two features are added to the notion: (1) something one will kill for and (2) something one willingly sends forth one's children to kill for and die for. Together with the notion of die-for-isms, these features may be interpreted as indicators of that which is of ultimate importance to groups, nations, and cultures.

In any event, since 1648, religion has not been important enough in Western culture to inspire the ultimate sacrifice—at least not on a large scale. Other institutions certainly have been, however: politics, the nation-state, economic models, secular ideals (liberty, solidarity, equality, representation, fair taxation, economic opportunity, and so on). Perhaps the "ultimate sacrifice test" best captures the notion of secularization. It certainly points to a major distinction between the pre-modern world and the modern world; and it seems also to suggest a similar distinction between the contemporary (postmodern) world and the modern world. We will leave it at that for now.

Suffice it to say, there are a variety of dates that one can use to mark the emergence of modern culture. Whatever that date may be, it is somewhat easier to specify the first great flowering of modernity. This would be the Enlightenment of the eighteenth century, marked by the three great revolutions of that century: the American, the French, and the Industrial. For working purposes, here, 1950 will mark the close of the modern period and the beginning of the postmodern. The year 1950 is chosen because it marks the point in Western culture when features identified as postmodern (to be described later in this chapter) begin to manifest in Western consciousness and material culture.

As already noted, postmodernity is the period that follows the modern and emerges in distinction to the modern. The list of contributors to theories of postmodernity is quite lengthy, although a number of major figures can be isolated. These include: Michel Foucault, Gilles Deleuze, Félix Guattari, David Harvey, Jean Baudrillard, Fredric Jameson, Jacques Derrida, Richard Rorty, and Jean-Francois Lyotard.

From the work of these and other theorists, certain critical features of postmodernity can be extracted. Four of special note are cited by Paul Heelas in his comments on the work of James Beckford:

> 1. A refusal to regard positivistic, rationalistic, instrumental criteria as the sole or exclusive standard of worthwhile knowledge. 2. A willingness to combine symbols from disparate codes or frameworks of meaning, even at the cost of disjunctions and eclecticism. 3. A celebration of spontaneity, fragmentation, superficiality, irony, and playfulness. 4. A willingness to abandon the search for over-arching or triumphalist myths, narratives, or frameworks of knowledge."[23]

Paul Lakeland also offers a list of four "essential postmodern issues" derived from Stephen White: "growing incredulity toward traditional metanarratives, new awareness of the costs of societal rationalization, the explosion of informational technologies, and the emergence of new social movements."[24] Lakeland continues, that "above all" postmodernity is a "challenge to the legacy of the Enlightenment," and further:

> Postmodernism is a frontal attack on [modernity]. It abandons the idea of ordered progress toward some goal, in which the autonomous human subject exercises the power of reason to subdue and arrange previously intractable nature toward that end. It is deeply suspicious of notions of universal reason, and it rejects all metaphysical or religious foundations, all "grand theory," all theoretical systems.[25]

Besides these features, other representative features are frequently considered in works on postmodernity. Adding these to those previously noted yields a list of elements, institutions, ideals, and forces that are commonly identified as distinctive manifestations of postmodernity:

Replacement of a techno-scientific worldview by a de-centered, a-historical worldview

The myth of pluralism

Historical, cultural, and ethical relativism

"The spirit of self-discovery"and the quest for personal meaning

The quest to "deconstruct" (one is tempted to say everything, but particularly) oppressive economic and political systems

Re-enchantment processes (New Age groups, Neo-Paganisms)

Religious resurgence (Fundamentalisms, Revival movements)

Participatory democracy and institutional decentralization

Expansion and technological sophistication of the mass media

Cyber-literacy

Radical individualism

Post-colonialism and globalization

Environmental degradation, ecological crises, climate change, and the emergence of the environmental movement

Eclipse of production-based capitalism with consumption-based capitalism

Technologization of the human environment and consciousness

The Green Revolution and explosive population growth

The rise of image-based communication

Blurring of distinctions between "high," "folk," and "popular" cultures, and the celebration of popular culture

Apocalypticism (religious, secular, ecological)

Rejection of repressive social compartmentalizations and dichotomies (gender, sexual choice, racial, ethnic)

Rejection of metanarratives (especially Eurocentric, androcentric, and religious)

Appreciation (and celebration) of irony, paradox, contradiction, rapid social change

In all of its many forms and definitions, postmodernity is understood as distinct from modernity. Thus, its beginning can be traced to events, movements, and persons seen as marking the end of the modern period, and specifically the end of the idealization of science, faith in the West's world-supremacy, beliefs in human perfectibility, and trust in an inexhaustible supply of natural resources. These are among the metanarratives that the postmodern worldview calls into question.

In this regard, the advent of postmodernity could be traced to decisive events that challenged the worldview or guiding principles of modernity. Candidates include the start or end of World War II (1939–1945), the Holocaust (1933–1945), the Vietnam War (1960s–1970s), Rachel Carson's *Silent Spring* (1962). As already noted, for working purposes (following Fredric Jameson), 1950 seems especially relevant, for it was around that time that the constellation of cultural features associated with postmodernity began to emerge in recognizable fashion. The fearful implications of atomic power began to be recognized and, with them, concerns about an apocalyptic nuclear war between the United States and the Soviet Union—an apocalypse initiated not by a transcendent deity but by human beings. With it came questions about the virtue of scientific exploration and doubts about human perfectibility. Suspicions were raised about the benefits of technology and the West's incredible manufacturing capacity, with the increasing awareness of the perils of industrial pollution and the relationship between industrial production and ecological destruction.

The world dominance of the West began to erode as the European nations gradually lost or abandoned their colonial holdings. This process was punctuated by events such as India gaining its independence from Britain, the French loss of Indochina and Algeria, and later the United States' loss in South Vietnam. The 1950s also saw the beginning of the ascent of Asian powers as challengers to the West's global hegemony. In this decade, Japan began its ascent as an industrial and technological challenger to the West, and China first appeared as a political and military challenger. The oil embargo of the early 1970s, which precipitated a severe recession in the West, only confirmed trends set in motion two decades before: the economies of the West were dependent on natural resources possessed by nations in other parts of the world—nations the West no longer could easily control.

Despite these challenges, the 1950s confirmed the United States' position as the world's greatest economic power even as powerful winds of change swept across its domestic cultural landscape. In this decade the Civil Rights movement was born, first with the Supreme Court decision, *Brown vs. Board of Education* (May 17, 1954), outlawing segregation in education. The next year, an African American seamstress (Rosa Parks) refused to give up her seat to a white man in Montgomery, Alabama, leading to a boycott of the city's buses led by a young preacher, the Reverend Dr. Martin Luther King, Jr. The Interstate Highway Act was passed in 1956, ending the dominance of the railroads as the primary method for interstate commerce and quickly making the entire nation accessible to individuals by automobile. Urban centers of the nation's great cities began to die as suburban communities developed, initially with William Jaird Levitt's planned community on Long Island in 1952—the first Levittown. Concurrent with the rise of suburbia came shopping centers. By 1957 there were 940; the number doubled by 1960, and doubled again by 1963.[26] A technology was perfected for reducing the size of air conditioning systems, and the mass production of these new "windowbox" air conditioners helped fuel a migration from northern industrial states to what came to be called "the Sun Belt." The GI Bill, targeted at veterans of World War II, resulted in dramatic increases in college enrollments and home construction. The veterans also started families, leading to the baby boom. Somewhat paradoxically, family planning was revolutionized with the perfection of an oral contraceptive product (a birth control pill) for women, which gave women control over not only their reproductive cycles but their career opportunities, as well. The 1950s also brought affordable televisions to most American homes, fast food and motel franchising, and the publication of the first issues of *Playboy* (1953) and *Sports Illustrated* (1954).

Capitalism also began to change at this time, as the production-based economic system of industrial capitalism began its transition to late capitalism's consumption-based system. During the 1950s, technological advances and manufacturing capacity transformed the economic order from one in which the focus was on production of commodities to one in which the focus was on their consumption. This shift from industrial/production-based systems is a major reason why some scholars equate the postmodern with the *postindustrial,* often using the latter term in place of postmodern. What is important to remember about this shift is that it is also reflected in culture, with the norms and values of a production-based system (which prizes labor, productivity, and the work ethic) being replaced by norms and values appropriate to a consumption-based system (which prizes recreation, consumption, and a leisure ethic).

As described by Fredric Jameson, in postmodern culture "commodity production [is based on the] frantic economic urgency of producing fresh waves of ever more novel-seeming goods (from clothing to airplanes), at ever greater rates of turnover," in which there is "an immense dilation of . . . the sphere of commodities . . . a commodity rush, our 'representations' of things tending to arouse an enthusiasm and a mood swing not necessarily inspired by the things themselves."[27] The "culture of consumption" is a dynamic force that, when "unleashed," consumes persons "to the point of being unable to imagine anything else."[28] Moreover, "we are *inside* the culture of the market and . . . the inner dynamic of the culture of consumption is an infernal machine from which one does not escape."[29]

Jameson's reading of consumption as the dominant characteristic of postmodern culture is affirmed and advanced by Jean Baudrillard. As noted by his critical exegete, Douglas Kellner, Baudrillard interprets postmodern culture as a culture of consumption in which "participation . . . requires systematic purchase and organization of domestic objects, fashion and so on into a system of organized codes and models."[30] In Baudrillard's own words:

> We have reached the point where "consumption" has grasped the whole of life, where all activities are connected in the same combi-

natorial mode. . . . In the phenomenology of consumption, this general climatization of life, goods, objects, services, behaviors and social relations represents the perfected, "consummated" stage of evolution which, through articulated networks of objects, ascends from pure and simple abundance to complete conditioning of action and time and finally to the systematic organization of ambience, which is characteristic of the drugstores, the shopping mall, or the modern airports in our futuristic cities.[31]

Kellner further interprets Baudrillard: "The consumer . . . cannot avoid the obligation to consume, because it is consumption that is the primary mode of social integration and the primary ethic and activity within the consumer society."[32] For him, consumerism requires "active labor, incessant curiosity and search for novelty, and conformity to the latest fads, products and demands to consume"; and through the acquisition of commodities "our entire society *communicates* and speaks of and to itself."[33] Finally, and most significantly, Baudrillard characterizes the consumer's mental attitude toward consumption as *"magical thought"*: "a miraculous mentality which rules everyday life, a primitive mentality in the sense that it is defined as a belief in the omnipotence of thoughts: in this case, belief in the omnipotence of signs."[34]

***

It is the assumption of this primer that Jameson and Baudrillard are essentially correct and that contemporary Western culture is accurately (if not conclusively) interpreted as one in which the consumption is a dominant feature and the consumption-based economic system a dominant institution. As I have argued elsewhere, consumption is, in fact, much more than merely a dominant feature, but actually a sacred obligation and the basis of postmodern religious life.[35] For purposes of this text, however, we will let it go with the more modest statement previously given, and also note that other institutions make fair claim to playing a dominant role in contemporary culture. These include politics and/or government, nationalism, the media, education, and science. Whatever institution(s) one chooses to specify as dominant, it is reasonable to recognize it (or them) as the source for the legitimation of the social order—much as religion was in earlier times. The concept of legitimation takes us back to the opening of Chapter 1, where the relationship of culture, society, and religion was sketched. As noted there:

For the vast bulk of human existence, religion has served as the primary source of foundational support for society. Sociologists refer to this sort of support as *legitimation,* by which they mean the process through which cultural understandings and social arrangements (large or small, oppressive or liberating, passive or assertive) are justified, especially in instances when they are questioned. Historically, religion has supplied society with the ultimate sort of legitimation by locating the social order in the context of a sacred (ultimate) order of existence.

What, then, is the role and status of religion in postmodern culture, where its traditional role in legitimating society seems to have been marginalized, if not replaced, by other cultural institutions? This is certainly a reasonable question in the context of the secularization thesis and its claims about modern culture; and to the degree that the secularization thesis is accepted, the reduced role and status of religion in modern culture seems clear enough. It was marginalized, its claims were desacralized, the world it described was disenchanted; and new institutions legitimated the social order, defining the world and justifying social conditions in ways that religion simply did not or could not. Those new institutions were the same as those cited here with reference to postmodern culture. Can the same claims be made today, however? Perhaps, but perhaps not. Perhaps it is politics and government, economics, science and technology, the media, and education (one or several, some or all) that are the dominant institutions of the contemporary West, defining the world and individual existence, supplying meaning and value, and legitimating society as a whole. Perhaps religion is out of the mix and out of the legitimation business today. Perhaps not.

Whether it is or is not is the subject of lively debate, and there is no end to the possible answers. Good arguments can be found on all sides, and several of the major positions have been reviewed in this chapter. It is left up to readers to consider the merits of the various positions and consult others as well. Suffice it to say, that just as contemporary Western culture (termed postmodern here) is nothing if not in the throes of vigorous transformation, the role and status of religion in this culture is likewise in the throes of change. What this change and transformation may mean to our understanding of religion and culture in the West, and with it the secularization thesis, is very much an open question. Central to this question, and part of what makes it particularly difficult to answer, is the reemergence of religion as a distinct cultural presence in the contemporary world. This reemergence, most often referred to as a *resurgence,* will be considered in the final section of this primer.

Endnotes

1. See their fine anthology on the "debate," with chapters from various perspectives, cited in the previous chapter. William H. Swatos, Jr., and Daniel V. A. Olson, *The Secularization Debate* (Lanham, MD: Rowman and Littlefield, 2000).
2. See my book, *The Sacred Santa: Religious Dimensions of Consumer Culture,* 3rd printing (Eugene, OR: Wipf Stock, 2008).
3. Berger, as cited in the previous chapter. Peter Berger, *The Sacred Canopy* (Garden City, NY: Anchor Books, 1969).
4. Peter Berger, *The Homeless Mind* (New York: Random House, 1973), and *The Heretical Imperative* (Garden City, NY: Anchor Press, 1979).
5. Bryan Wilson, *Religion in Secular Society* (London: Watts, 1969) and *Contemporary Transformations of Religion* (Oxford: Oxford University Press, 1976).
6. Bryan Wilson, "The Secularization Thesis: Criticisms and Rebuttals," in *Secularization and Social Integration: Papers in Honor of Karel Dobbelaere,* eds. Rudi Laermans, Bryan Wilson, and Jacques Billiet (Leuven, Netherlands: Leuvern University Press, 1998), 45–66.
7. Karel Dobbelaere, "Secularization: A Multi-Dimensional Concept," in *Current Sociology* 29 (1981): 1–213.
8. Marcel Gauchet, *The Disenchantment of the World: A Political History of Religion,* trans. Oscar Burge (Princeton, NJ: Princeton University Press, 1997).
9. Harvey Cox, *The Secular City* (New York: Macmillan, 1965).
10. Steve Bruce, *Religion in the Modern World: From Cathedrals to Cults* (Oxford: Oxford University Press, 1996), and *God Is Dead: Secularization in the West* (Oxford: Blackwell, 2002).
11. For representative works, see Grace Davie, The Sociology of Religion (Los Angeles: Sage, 2007), esp chap. 12; Yves Lambert, "Religion in Modernity as a New Axial Age," in The Secularization Debate, ed. Swatos and Daniel V.A. Olson (Lanham, MD: Rowman and Littlefield, 2000), 95-125; Vincent P. Pecora, Secularization and Cultural Criticism (Chicago: University of Chicago Press, 2006); and Charles Taylor, A Secular Age (Cambridge, MA: The Belknap Press of Harvard University Press, 2007), esp. chap. 1 and 15.
12. David Martin, "Towards Eliminating the Concept of Secularization," in *Penguin Survey of the Social Sciences,* ed. Julius Gould (Baltimore: Penguin, 1965), 169–182.
13. David Martin, *A General Theory of Secularization* (Oxford: Blackwell, 1978), "The Secularization Issue: Prospect and Retrospect" in *British Journal of Sociology,* 42 (1991): 466–474, and *On Secularization: Towards a Revised General Theory* (Burlington, VT: Ashgate, 2005).
14. Quotations of Hadden from Jeffrey K. Hadden, "Toward Desacralizing Secularization," *Social Forces,* 65 (1987): 587–611, as given in Swatos and Kevin Christiano, "Secularization Theory: The Course of a Concept," 2.

15. Rodney Stark, "Secularization, R.I.P.," in *Sociology of Religion*, 60 (1999): 249–270. Also in Swatos and Christiano, 41–66.
16. Davie, 69.
17. Rodney Stark and William S. Bainbridge, *The Future of Religion: Secularization, Revival, and Cult Formation* (Berkeley: University of California Press, 1985), 3. Italics are mine.
18. Steve Bruce, *Religion in the Modern World*, 188–190. Bruce cites another critique of Stark and Bainbridge; see Roy Wallis and Steve Bruce, "The Stark-Bainbridge Theory of Religion: A Critical Analysis and Counter-Proposals," *Sociological Analysis*, 45 (1984): 11–27.
19. Rodney Stark and Laurence Iannaccone, "A Supply-side Reinterpretation of the 'Secularization of Europe,'" in *Journal for the Scientific Study of Religion* 33 (1994): 230–252; and Stark and Roger Finke, *Acts of Faith* (Berkeley: University of California Press, 2000).
20. Peter Berger, ed., *The Desecularization of the World: Resurgent Religion and World Politics* (Grand Rapids, MI: Eerdmans, 1999).
21. Ibid., 2.
22. Roger Corless, "Building on Eliade's Magnificent Failure," in *Changing Religious Worlds: The Meaning and End of Mircea Eliade*, ed. Bryan Rennie (Albany: State University Press of New York, 2001), 9. Corless cites Ninian Smart, *Beyond Ideology: Religion and the Future of Western Civilization* (San Francisco: Harper and Row, 1981), especially chapter 7.
23. James Beckford, "Religion, Modernity and Post-Modernity," in *Religion: Contemporary Issues*, ed. Bryan Wilson, as cited by Paul Heelas, "Introduction: On Differentiation and Dedifferentiation," in *Religion, Modernity and Post Modernity*, ed. Paul Heelas, (Oxford: Blackwell, 1998), 4.
24. Stephen White, *Political Theory and Postmodernism* (Cambridge: Cambridge University Press, 1991), as cited by Paul Lakeland, *Postmodernity: Christian Identity in a Fragmented Age* (Minneapolis: Fortress Press, 1997), xi.
25. Lakeland, xii.
26. Lizabeth Cohen, *A Consumer's Republic* (New York: Alfred A. Knopf, 2003), 258.
27. Fredric Jameson, *Postmodernism, or The Cultural Logic of Late Capitalism* (Durham, NC: Duke University Press, 1991), 5, x.
28. Ibid., 207.
29. Ibid., 206.
30. Douglas Kellner, *Jean Baudrillard: From Marxism to Postmodernism and Beyond* (Stanford, CA: Stanford University Press, 1989), 13.
31. Ibid., selection from Jean Baudrillard, *Selected Writings*, ed. Mark Poster (Cambridge and Palo Alto: Polity Press and Stanford University Press, 1988), 33.
32. Ibid., 16.
33. Ibid.
34. Ibid., 14. From Baudrillard, *La société de consommation* (Paris: Gallimard, 1970), 27 (Kellner's translation of passage).
35. See note 2.

Coda

The Question of
Religious Resurgence
in the Contemporary West

Religious resurgence is accelerating today, and religion in the contemporary West (and indeed the world) is a more powerful presence in culture than it has been since the seventeenth century. Begun in the latter part of the twentieth century, religious resurgence is now a well-established (if not widely recognized) feature of contemporary cultures. Where once globalization promoted secularization, today it can be argued that it promotes religious resurgence.

In the United States, religion openly challenges the nation's secular ideals more vigorously than ever before in the nation's history. In the past decade, there have been major disputes over the teaching of "creation science," legal battles taken to the Supreme Court over posting the Ten Commandments in government buildings, state and national struggles over the right of same-sex partners to marry, expansion of public funding for religious schools, religiously inspired initiatives to restrict the "reproductive rights" of women, and religiously motivated government policies funding "faith-based initiatives" and banning stem cell research. Even as the ecological crisis worsened and the impact of climate change on human cultures became ever more vivid and powerful, religious persons were among those most likely to reject scientific findings on the issue and even deny the reality of climate change.[1]

In contemporary popular culture, the significance of religion is reflected in the recent or continuing success of a variety of different religious cultural expressions. These include the appearance of evangelical megachurches; widespread distribution of the Islamic State's slick social media productions, widening interest in new religions, such as Pentecostalism, New Thought, Jehovah's Witnesses, and Scientology (to name a few); the increasing popularity of non-Western religions and religious practices (for example, various forms of Buddhism and Hinduism, yoga, meditation rituals, tai chi, and feng shui); the penetration of religion into mainstream media-culture, including the *Left Behind* series, hit movies like *The Passion of the Christ, Kingdom of Heaven, Avatar,* and *Exodus: Gods and Kings*; and the routine appearance of religion on TV programs, such as *The Simpsons* and *South Park.*

Worldwide, the early twenty-first century has also witnessed a dramatic increase in violence motivated by religious beliefs. Instances of religious-inspired violence during this time period are numerous, troubling, and easy to research.

Certainly, the most well-known recent instance of religious-inspired violence occurred on September 11, 2001. On the morning of that day, persons associated with a militant religious organization destroyed the iconic twin towers and other structures of the World Trade Center in New York City. As a result, the United States invaded and took control of the nation of Afghanistan, ousting a religious-based government, and initiating a "War on Terror." As part of this war, the United States attacked Afghanistan, quickly suppressed oppositional forces, and replaced the religious-inspired government with a secular democracy. Shortly after taking control of Afghanistan, the United States invaded Iraq, later justifying the action as part of the War on Terror. After the defeat of oppositional forces, the United States installed a secular democracy, fracturing the sacred legitmation of the culture, and reawakening centuries-old religious tensions. The result was an eruption of intense religious violence, plunging the nation into near anomy, and precipitating the rise of a militant religion-inspired international community: The Islamic State (or, the Islamic State in Iraq and the Levant [ISIL, for short]).

As of this writing (2015), ISIL and related groups such as Boko Haram in Nigeria and al-Shabaab in East Africa stand in violent defiance of the Western culture, and not incidentally the ideals of secularization – e.g., capitalism, democracy, pluralism, gender equality. Likewise, America and other Western nations have responded and continue to respond with violence against these religiously motivated groups. This violence takes many forms: suicide bombings have been frequent but so, too, have been "surgical" and not-so-surgical bombings by drones, guided missiles, attack aircraft, and a host of other instruments of death and destruction. Innocents die from both types of bombing. So does innocence. Atrocities have occurred on all sides and religious hate crimes have increased dramatically throughout the world.

It may perhaps be a stretch to identify this violent struggle between Western military forces and militants inspired by religion as a religious war, but it is naive to ignore its religious features. Arguably, the war contains a religious dynamic and, although most in the West (especially the United States), would reject the notion that the actions of the United States are in any way religious or religiously motivated, the same cannot be said about those the United States is relentlessly attacking. Moreover, it might be well to remember that when religion is understood in a cosmological context (as sketched in the opening chapter), the sacred is embedded within the culture itself, sanctifying its norms and values, and sacralizing its way of life. When considered in this way, it is less far-fetched to suggest that there is a religious dimension in the violent actions of the United States against its more explicitly religious adversaries.

What is certainly evident is that events summarized here indicate that for many in the world today religion has again become a justification for violence and, for some, a Corless-Smart "die-for-ism." As suggested earlier, a *die-for-ism* is better understood as a kill-for-ism as well as a die-for-ism, and a force legitimating and celebrating the sacrifice of one's children to the business of killing and dying. It is not just religion, however, that is classified in this category. The more established and accepted institutions that have inspired killing and dying on a massive, culturally supported scale since the dawn of modernity are still highly functional—government, economics, nationalism, the media.

What is worth our attention today is religion again being listed among these institutions; and it is perhaps for this reason, as much as any other, that religious violence is so chilling to many in the West. To Westerners, religiously motivated violence is absurd; it is atavistic, medieval, unthinkable, irrational, uncivilized. It is certainly not modern as the concept has been presented here, but it might very well be *postmodern* as that concept has been described.

For three and a half centuries, the West has developed a culture in which religion is marginalized, privatized, and domesticated— anything but a kill-and-die-for-ism. Therefore, when religion enters the public sphere in an assertive manner, especially one that includes challenges to the status quo of secular culture, many in the West are alarmed. When this challenge includes violence in the name of religion, for many it is simply incomprehensible—and terrifying. I might also suggest that it is enormously fascinating. It is scary and captivating, repulsive and riveting, eerie and intriguing.[2]

In short, until recent events forced a reconsideration of the world, Western culture seemed to have largely confirmed Nietzsche's claim that God was dead and the general assumptions of the secularization thesis. This is not to say that vast numbers of Westerners (especially Americans) do not value religion—hardly. America remains one of the most religious nations in the world, and perhaps the most religiously diverse culture in human history. It simply means that until fairly recent times, religion has generally functioned as an individual and private concern, and religious institutions have generally accepted their own marginalization while accommodating themselves to religious tolerance predicated on cultural pluralism. This is consistent with the standard account of the secularization thesis. Certainly there have been exceptions—for example: the early persecutions of the Latter Day Saints and the Saints' resistance to those persecutions; the opposition to civil and medical authorities by Jehovah's Witnesses and Christian Science; and challenges brought against repressive government practices in the name of religion by the Reverend Dr. Martin Luther King, Jr., and Malcolm X. These, and other moments in American history, are notable, but they stand out because they have been exceptions to the cultural norms of America and the West—until recently. What this recent change tells us brings us back again to the status of religion in contemporary culture.

I think the question is best contextualized relative to the secularization thesis, for the status of religion is related to the status of the thesis that explains its marginalization. As a result, if the continued viability of the standard account of the secularization thesis is accepted, religion can be understood as marginalized and its significance to contemporary culture not appreciably different than it was to modern culture. Those who are less committed to the thesis or entertain alternative interpretations will less readily agree; and those who reject the thesis will also most likely object to the dismissal of religion as a critical force in postmodern culture. There are good arguments on both sides and various positions in between.

***

To those who maintain the viability of the secularization thesis, the resurgence of religion in the contemporary world is a case where looks can be deceiving. For them, postmodern culture (if they even acknowledge it as a valid category) is at best an extension of modern culture. There is no clear break, as recognized by those who identify a postmodern culture in distinction to the modern. If there is such a break, it does not affect secularization. The status of religion is still that of a marginalized institution; what power it has is secondary to more dominant institutions (e.g., politics, economics, the media). This position can face claims of a religious resurgence without apology or compromise.

In response to arguments that the secularization thesis is challenged by the increased power, visibility, and acceptance of religion (from political action and militancy to megachurches, new religions, and media penetration), proponents can offer a variety of rebuttals. Perhaps the most telling is that the resurgence of religion can be entirely accounted for in the context of the thesis itself. The thesis, after all, does not claim that religion will disappear but, rather, that it ceases to be the foundational institution within a culture system. The thesis accounts for the decline of religion and its eclipse by other institutions as the primary source of legitimation for society and *truth* for individuals. It is certainly possible to sustain the secularization thesis and still acknowledge the significance of the role of religion in the lives of human beings in the world today. As Bruce observes, the thesis, "is a set of associated explanations rather than a single theory," which "does not require secularization to be universal or even," and further, "it does not suppose the course of history to be smooth and hence is not refuted by humps and lumps; and it does not suppose that the only alternative to religion is irreligion."[3] For Bruce and other defenders of the thesis, the apparent resurgence of religion today is one of these "humps and lumps."

The very resistance of religion to secularizing forces indicates the profound presence of secularization and its dominance over culture. Moreover, the forms of resistance that religion takes (de-modernization or counter-modernization) are themselves co-opted by secularization itself. Religion-qua-religion is not resurgent, according to proponents; what has happened is that religions (or at least selected religious claims) have become politicized and entered the political arena, becoming political movements, political parties, political ideologies. In doing so, they lose their primary identity as religions. What is meaningful about such movements, and what makes them successful, is not their religious claims but their political acumen; their use of the media, their bureaucratic structures, their gaining control of government structures, their repression of opposition, their coalition building, and so on. In short, their success is not due to their identity as religions but their ability to win at the game of politics. Thus, they are most accurately classified as political movements—albeit, ones that make use of religion.

Religious militancy fares no better against the secularization rebuttal. In fact, it probably is easier to account for. The rebuttal follows the same strategy as the political rebuttal and builds on it. First co-opted by politics, religion is further co-opted by militants within the political community. For a group to gain political power by the use of violence does not make the group or movement any more or less religious, even if the use of rhetoric by the group includes ample quantities of religious language and assertions of religious justification. The goal is the secular treasure of political power: the control of government, the economy, the bureaucratic machinery of the state.

What religionists are ultimately striving for are secular, political ideals—freedom, self-determination, economic independence, nationalism, social equality, and so on. Religious rhetoric has great value in such pursuits, but the rhetoric is serving other ends than those of the religion from which they have been appropriated.

Another tactic that secularization proponents might use would be to observe that the secularization thesis is offered as an account for religion in the modern world and the so-called religious resurgence appears largely confined to parts of the world that are best classified as pre-modern. Modernity (as summarized in Chapter 4) necessarily brings with it secularization, and in modern cultures there is no indication that religion is resurgent in any meaningful sense—hence, the irrationality to Westerners of martyr bombing and other expressions of religious violence. By contrast, to the degree that religion is genuinely resurgent and used as a justification for violence, it is only occurring in those parts of the world that are pre-modern in their cultural orientation. This is entirely to be expected in pre-modern cultures—just as we saw in the pre-modern West prior to 1648 and the end of the Thirty Years' War. Perhaps there is a resurgence of religion in parts of the world that have recently become independent of direct Western control, but this resurgence is not apparent in the West itself.

The claim that the success of a variety of different religious expressions (e.g., megachurches, new religions, television programming, and religious movies) challenges the secularization thesis can also be rebutted by its advocates. Again, the tactic would be to remind critics that the thesis does not mandate the elimination of religion but "a long-term decline in the power, popularity and prestige of religious beliefs and rituals."[4] It also allows for Bruce's "humps and lumps" that include megachurches, new religions, *Avatar*, and *Exodus*. Further, and this more or less follows Bruce, these phenomena can hardly count against the secularization thesis because they (like all the other seeming challenges) are predicated on social features specifically accounted for by secularization.

In brief, these religious phenomena are successful not because religion dominates culture and its institutions, but precisely because it does not. They are successful because they appeal to individuals-qua-individuals. There is no binding religious obligation to go to the megachurch, read a book in the *Left Behind* series, or join a new religion. Religion does not work that way any more, according to the secularization thesis. Instead, individuals make personal choices about how they desire to spend their time and money. Some, perhaps many, may opt to go to church; and if they have not gone in a while, megachurches may have significant appeal. They have excellent marketing and good management, they are lively and upbeat, and they make few compelling demands on participants. Others might opt to sleep in, go to work for some overtime pay, read the paper, or get ready for some football. Churches (mega or otherwise) are not the only game in town.

When it comes to movies, *The Passion of the Christ* competed with other movies when it was initially released and continues to compete for viewers on DVD. It was a huge box office hit and the highest grossing R-rated movie ever released—a success in a culture where success is measured by income. Said another way, it maximized viewership within its target demographic. Again, its success does not count against the secularization thesis any more than the success of megachurches. Individuals made personal choices to see the film (or not); and although many Christians did see it, their decision to do so was not due to Christianity's dominance of American culture and its institutions. It was due to Hollywood, the reputation of the director, the buzz in the media, and the positive promotion it received at local religious communities. After a few weeks in the spotlight, its popularity faded. It also generated public opposition and negative publicity for its director, predicated precisely on its religious features. Similar rebuttals could be offered for the popularity of new religions, East and South Asian religions and religious practices, and TV programs that include religious characters and storylines. None indicate any particular erosion of secularization; all are accounted for within the framework of the thesis. If they are meaningful at all, they are at best a hump or a lump.

***

By contrast, the status of religion in contemporary culture can be interpreted as representing something a bit more than a hump or a bump within the standard account of the secularization thesis. In fact, the resurgence of religion can be taken as offering a clear challenge to the thesis. There appear to be two general approaches to constructing such a challenge: the "usual suspects" approach, and the "neo-cosmological" approach.

Chapter 4 considered traditional challenges to the thesis, and readers may benefit from reviewing them at this time. These traditional challenges (e.g., "the golden age argument," the ideological bias argument, and RCT) often include or develop arguments using the *usual suspects* approach. In this instance, the *usual suspects* are long-established historical religions, modern variations on these religions, or new religious movements. In whatever ways the secularization thesis is deemed deficient (see Chapter 4 for details on the claimed deficiencies), the resurgence of rather classical forms of religion is offered as supporting evidence against the thesis. Examples of this approach can be found in the work of Jeffrey K. Hadden, Gilles Kepel, Mark Juergensmeyer, and especially Rodney Stark and William Bainbridge's *The Future of Religion* and Peter Berger's *The Desecularization of the World.*[5]

In these interpretations, the usual suspects are understood in fairly straightforward ways, typically using or implying substantive definitions, including a belief in a supernatural ultimate power. The resurgence of religion in these instances refers to religions that most people would readily recognize as religion. If not the historic world religions themselves, those included in these studies are recent variations of the historic religions. Also included are new religious movements that may or may not have clear affinities with historical religions but nonetheless share features that identify them as religions. More specifically, a sampling of the usual suspects cited as an example of contemporary religious vitality that counts against the secularization thesis includes the following rather diverse collection of groups and movements:

al-Qaeda
al-Shabaab
Aum Shinrikyo
Boko Haram
the Bharatiya Janata Party
the Branch Davidians
the Catholic Charismatic movement
the Free Tibet movement
Fundamentalisms and resurgence movements in various traditions
Gush Emunim
Hamas
ISIL
Jama'at al Tabligh
Latter Day Saints

Liberation Theology
the Lubavitch
The Moral Majority
the New Age movement
Pentecostalism
Scientology
the Taliban

The groups listed here are only a sampling representing various religious traditions. They cover a wide spectrum of social activism. Some embrace violence; others do not. Some are politically active; others are not. What they have in common is their identification as examples of a religious resurgence brought forward as challenges to the secularization thesis. Rather than declining or existing as marginal institutions, religions today vigorously vie with secular institutions for power and authority in the world and in the lives of individuals. Together these groups and movements, along with countless others, substantiate Berger's claim that the contemporary world "is as furiously religious as it ever was, and in some places more so than ever," and "the whole body of literature by historians and social scientists loosely labeled 'secularization theory' is essentially mistaken."[6] As already outlined, there are ample rebuttals to this claim.

In addition to the usual suspects approach, challenges to the secularization thesis can be developed using what can be termed the *neo-cosmological* approach. Rather than claiming the thesis is invalidated by the resurgence of religion in its more recognizable guise, the neo-cosmological approach, on the whole, accepts the basic premise of the thesis but observes that its relevance is restricted to religions as traditionally conceived (i.e., those earlier described as transcendental). These religions, after all, are the systems most readily captured in substantive definitions with their stress typically on supernatural concepts of ultimate power. In this regard, the strongest proponent of the secularization thesis (Steve Bruce) and one of its most ardent critics (Rodney Stark) both argue for and deploy substantive definitions of religion, which include belief in a supernatural ultimate power. Further, both reject functionalist definitions as too broad.

In contrast to the usual suspects approach, the neo-cosmological approach typically uses functional definitions and does not minimize or marginalize the religious character of what typically is presented as secular culture. Rather than relegating religion to its classical forms and analyzing it in the context of its reduced status in contemporary culture, neo-cosmological theories recognize religious features in seemingly secular institutions and processes. For them, the religious expressions of contemporary culture may well be quite different from what ordinarily passes for religion; and institutions usually recognized as religious may neither be the dominant material embodiments of contemporary religiosity nor the belief systems that accurately serve to mediate human relations with the sacred.

From the neo-cosmological standpoint, institutions and communities normally classified as religion (namely, the usual suspects) face serious challenges from alternative forms of religiosity that are at once uniquely contemporary in form and function while also being incredibly ancient in foundational structure. These alternative forms of religious expression are distinctly different from the traditional religions with which culture is most familiar. Where traditional religions are transcendental (in their locus of the sacred) and anthropological (in their locus of human meaning and value), the alternative religions with which they compete today are cosmological (in their locus of the sacred) and sociological (in their locus of human meaning and value).

The contours of the cosmological worldview (outlined in earlier chapters) are the theoretic bases for neo-cosmological theories. In ancient cosmological societies, which depended on the cycles of nature and fertility of the natural environment, nature and the natural environment were the ground of the sacred—the ground of ultimate concern, awe and fascination, dread, and enchantment. Today, however, new elements have replaced nature as the sacred ground and locus of ultimate concern. As explained nicely by Jacques Ellul: "The novelty of our era is that man's deepest experience is no longer with nature. . . . Hence [nature] is no longer the inciter and place of the sacred."[7] Instead, in his analysis, "the modern western technical and scientific world is a sacral world" and "technology is the god who saves."[8] In essence, in today's world, for Ellul, technology has come to occupy a place analogous to that of nature in antiquity. Ellul's identification of technology as the sacred is one example of the neo-cosmological approach. Other possibilities are the nation-state (which Ellul also cites as an expression of the sacred), economics, and science.

Whatever the sacred may be (in antiquity or today), it is the source of ultimate power and ultimate dread, what Otto would call the *mysterium tremendum et fascinans;*[9] and so, like nature in antiquity, the sacred of today elicits a religious response. As with the cosmological attitude of yore, modern cosmological religious expressions seek to relate persons and all of culture to the source of sacred power. Just as the ancient cosmological religions utilized myth and ritual to establish and legitimate this relationship, so, too, do modern cosmological religions; but since the source of sacred power has changed, so, too, have the myths and rituals. Where once the myths told of a sacred time of ancestors and heroes, gods of nature and fertility, today they tell us of the sacred origins and mysterious processes of technology, the nation-state, economics, science, or some other power identified as the sacred. For their part, rituals relate us to the sacred through uniquely patterned activities that vivify the myths.

As a result, what have come to function as religions in contemporary society are the seemingly secular institutions that articulate myths and embody rituals that relate culture to the sacred forces of today. In this sense, some of the more obvious options for contemporary neo-cosmological religions are politics, nationalism, the media, and consumerism—even sports and entertainment might qualify. Proponents of this approach, thus, do not so much reject the secularization thesis as they modify it, arguing that the secular institutions that eclipsed religion beginning in the modern period have themselves become sacred mediators; vehicles through which society is located in a cosmic (sacred) frame of reference—the nation, the economy, technology. In short, the seemingly secular has become the functionally religious.

***

As noted at the close of the last chapter, the status of religion in the contemporary West, and with it the secularization thesis, is an open question. The question has engendered a wide variety of answers, a sampling of which have been presented in this primer. They are not the only answers, (this is a primer, after all), but they are, to my mind, among the better ones (both pro and con). They have the additional merit of being generally accessible to educated readers.

As good as these answers are, I contend that none is authoritative and that, at present, there is no conclusive answer to the question before us. Further, I suggest that we should be suspicious of answers proffered as such. We are wise, however, to familiarize ourselves with as many answers as possible, consider how they are developed and determine to what ends they are used. We are also well served by initially approaching the responses in a neutral manner, without allowing personal biases to cloud our evaluation.

Most of all, in evaluating any interpretation of religion in contemporary culture, a (if not *the*) central concern should be the value of its contribution to our individual and collective understanding of both religion and culture. Such value may be measured by consideration of the adequacy, coherence, relevancy, and helpfulness of the interpretation. Each should be subjected to a test based on four questions: Does it offer an adequate account of religion and culture; is it coherent (clearly organized and internally consistent); is it conversant with relevant sources; and does it genuinely help us better understand the phenomena it purports to interpret? If we can offer a positive judgment in each of these areas, we have a good basis for beginning our critical evaluation of the strengths and weakness of the interpretation and its usefulness to the specific concerns of our particular research.

***

As of 2015, it is clear that the religious resurgence of the last decades of the twentieth century is continuing on into the twenty-first – and, if anything, it is accelerating. Across the globe, religion is again defining individuals, inspiring action, and challenging the norms of secular culture. In the West, three centuries of secularization may well be coming to an end; and religion's ancient, atavistic moods and myths are again surfacing in the turbulence of contemporary culture. In other parts of the world, the West's secular ideals are being forcibly and often violently rejected in favor of pre-modern religious principles.

Religious violence is escalating and religious inspiration for violence is on the rise. A day does not pass when there is not a report of religion-inspired violence – sometimes several. It is often bombings (suicide and otherwise), but it also includes military conflict, beheadings, torture tales, kidnappings, and violent attacks on religious communities and individuals. 2014 alone saw the rise of ISIL in West Asia, and the dramatic expansion of Boko Haram in Nigeria, and al-Shabaab in East Africa. It also saw a massive victory by an American political party that caters to religious conservatives and promotes legislation favoring religious communities.

Today, the West is engaged in violent struggle against religiously motivated groups from Africa through West Asia and as far as Central Asia. Although the West may not view this as a religious struggle (secure in its secularized cultural consciousness), it certainly can be interpreted that way – especially when deploying the concept of neo-cosmological religion. Besides this, the adverse impacts of anthropogenic climate change are increasing, becoming ever more obvious, even to skeptics and climate-change deniers. The challenge of climate change may also not appear to be religious in character, but again, it is important to remember that climate change (like militant religious communities) is a direct and powerful assault on the ideals of contemporary Western culture – calling into question the sacred legitimation of that culture on the basis of science, technology, capitalism, mass-consumption, and personal freedom.

In the face of these challenges, many Westerners are turning to more traditional forms of religion or embracing political views rooted in religious beliefs or functionally religious in character.

It is difficult to project with even vague certainty the course of religion and culture in the West over the rest of the twenty-first century – or over the next decade. Enormous challenges confront the world, and tremendous changes are sweeping over the planet. Traditional forms of religion are morphing rapidly, and neo-cosmological religions are appearing around the world. The questions we have long asked about religion and culture are still the same: what is the sacred, what is the Ultimate Power, tell me your myths, show me your rituals, on what principles and practices is your culture legitimated, what will you die for? These old questions persist. The tricky part is not the questions, it is clearly and distinctly hearing the answers, and discovering the meanings embedded in those answers. This primer has not pretended to answer the questions, only to introduce the questions and frame them in the proper context. If answers and meanings come from that, all the better, but that is beyond the aim of this text – but not beyond its hope.

Endnotes

1. For data and reports, see (for example): Randal S. Olson, "Who Are the Climate Change Deniers?" Independent Researcher, September 13, 2014. http://www.randalolson.com/2014/09/13/who-are-the-climate-change-deniers/
    Chris Mooney, "Why Climate Change Skeptics and Evolution Deniers Joined Forces, *Mother Jones*, November 27, 2013. http://www.motherjones.com/blue-marble/2013/11/why-climate-change-skeptics-evolution-deniers-joined-forces
    Katherine Stewart, "How the Religious Right Is Fueling Climate Change Denial," *The Guardian*, November 5, 2012. http://www.alternet.org/environment/how-religious-right-fueling-climate-change-denial

2. In this regard, it has certain affinities with Otto's concept of religious experience as *mysterium tremendum et fascinans*—the wholly other that at once threatens and fascinates. The best example of this sort of affinity was the reaction of Americans to the events of September 11, 2001, particularly the ritual TV viewing that ensued. See Rudolf Otto, *The Idea of the Holy*, trans. John H. Harvey (London: Oxford University Press, 1982), 13–40.

3. Steve Bruce, *God Is Dead: Secularization in the West* (Oxford: Blackwell, 2002), 43–44.
4. Ibid.
5. See Jeffrey K. Hadden, "Toward Desacralizing Secularization Theory," in *Social Forces* 65:3 (1987), 587–561; Gilles Kepel, *The Revenge of God: The Resurgence of Islam, Christianity and Judaism in the Modern World,* trans. Alan Braley (University Park: The Pennsylvania State University Press, 1994); Mark Juergensmeyer, *Terror in the Mind of God: The Global Rise of Religious Violence* (Berkeley: University of California Press, 2000); Rodney Stark and William S. Bainbridge, *The Future of Religion: Secularization, Revival, and Cult Formation* (Berkeley: University of California Press, 1985); and Peter Berger, ed., *The Desecularization of the World: Resurgent Religion and World Politics* (Grand Rapids, MI: Eerdmans, 1999).
6. Berger, 2.
7. Jacques Ellul, *The New Demons,* trans. C. Edward Hopkin (New York: Seaburyp Press, 1975), 66.
8. Ibid., 70, 73.
9. See note 1.

Appendix 1
The Dialogue Decalogue

Ground Rules for Interreligious, Interideological Dialogue

Leonard Swidler

Dialogue is a conversation on a common subject between two or more persons with differing views, the primary purpose of which is for each participant to learn from the other so that he or she can change and grow. This very definition of dialogue embodies the first commandment of dialogue.

In the religious-ideological sphere in the past, we came together to discuss with those differing with us, for example, Catholics with Protestants, either to defeat an opponent, or to learn about an opponent so as to deal more effectively with him or her, or at best to negotiate with him or her. If we faced each other at all, it was in confrontation—sometimes more openly polemically, sometimes more subtly so, but always with the ultimate goal of defeating the other, because we were convinced that we alone had the absolute truth.

But dialogue is not debate. In dialogue each partner must listen to the other as openly and sympathetically as he or she can in an attempt to understand the other's position as precisely and, as it were, as much from within, as possible. Such an attitude automatically includes the assumption that at any point we might find the partner's position so persuasive that, if we would act with integrity, we would have to change, and change can be disturbing.

We are here, of course, speaking of a specific kind of dialogue, an interreligious, interideological dialogue. To have such, it is not sufficient that the dialogue partners discuss a religious-ideological subject, that is, the meaning of life and how to live accordingly. Rather, they must come to the dialogue as persons somehow significantly identified with a religious or ideological community. If I were neither a Christian nor a Marxist, for example, I could not participate as a

From *Journal of Ecumenical Studies,* Winter 1983 (20:1) by Leonard Swidler. Copyright © 1984 by *Journal of Ecumenical Studies.* Reprinted with permission.

"partner" in Christian-Marxist dialogue, though I might listen in, ask some questions for information, and make some helpful comments.

It is obvious that interreligious, interideological dialogue is something new under the sun. We could not conceive of it, let alone do it in the past. How, then, can we effectively engage in this new thing? The following are some basic ground rules, or "commandments," of interreligious, interideological dialogue that must be observed if dialogue is actually to take place. These are not theoretical rules, or commandments given from "on high," but ones that have been learned from hard experience.

FIRST COMMANDMENT: *The primary purpose of dialogue is to learn, that is, to change and grow in the perception and understanding of reality, and then to act accordingly.* Minimally, the very fact that I learn that my dialogue partner believes "this" rather than "that" proportionally changes my attitude toward her; and a change in my attitude is a significant change in me. We enter into dialogue so that we can learn, change, and grow, not so we can force change on the *other,* as one hopes to do in debate—a hope realized in inverse proportion to the frequency and ferocity with which debate is entered into. On the other hand, because in dialogue *each* partner comes with the intention of learning and changing herself, one's partner in fact will also change. Thus the goal of debate, and much more, is accomplished far more effectively by dialogue.

SECOND COMMANDMENT: *Interreligious, interideological dialogue must be a two-sided project—within each religious or ideological community and between religious or ideological communities.* Because of the "corporate" nature of interreligious dialogue, and since the primary goal of dialogue is that each partner learn and change himself, it is also necessary that each participant enter into dialogue not only with his partner across the faith line—the Lutheran with the Anglican, for example—but also with his coreligionists, with his fellow Lutherans, to share with them the fruits of the interreligious dialogue. Only thus can the whole community eventually learn and change, moving toward an ever more perceptive insight into reality.

THIRD COMMANDMENT: *Each participant must come to the dialogue with complete honesty and sincerity.* It should be made clear in what direction the major and minor thrusts of the tradition move, what the future shifts might be, and, if necessary, where the participant has difficulties with her own tradition. No false fronts have any place in dialogue.

Conversely—each participant must assume a similar complete honesty and sincerity in the other partners. Not only will the absence of sincerity prevent dialogue from happening, but the absence of the assumption of the partner's sincerity will do so as well. In brief: no trust, no dialogue.

FOURTH COMMANDMENT: *In interreligious, interideological dialogue we must not compare our ideals with our partner's practice,* but rather our ideals with our partner's ideals, our practice with our partner's practice.

FIFTH COMMANDMENT: *Each participant must define himself.* Only the Jew, for example, can define what it means to be a Jew. The rest can only describe what it looks like from the outside. Moreover, because dialogue is a dynamic medium, as each participant learns, he will change and hence continually deepen, expand, and modify his self-definition as a Jew—being careful to remain in constant dialogue with fellow Jews. Thus it is mandatory that each dialogue partner define what it means to be an authentic member of his own tradition.

Conversely—the one interpreted must be able to recognize herself in the interpretation. This is the golden rule of interreligious hermeneutics, as has been often reiterated by the "apostle of interreligious dialogue," Raimundo Panikkar. For the sake of understanding, each dialogue participant will naturally attempt to express for herself what she thinks is the meaning of the partner's statement; the partner must be able to recognize herself in that expression. The advocate of "a world theology," Wilfred Cantwell Smith, would add that the expression must also be verifiable by critical observers who are not involved.

SIXTH COMMANDMENT: *Each participant must come to the dialogue with no hard-and-fast assumptions as to where the points of disagreement are.* Rather, each partner should not only listen to the other partner with openness and sympathy but also attempt to agree with the dialogue partner as far as is possible while still maintaining integrity with his own tradition; where he absolutely can agree no further without violating his own integrity, precisely there is the real point of disagreement—which most often turns out to be different from the point of disagreement that was falsely assumed ahead of time.

SEVENTH COMMANDMENT: *Dialogue can take place only between equals,* or *par cum pari* as Vatican II put it. Both must come to learn from each other. Therefore, if, for example, the Muslim views Hinduism as inferior, or if the Hindu views Islam as inferior, there will be no dialogue. If authentic interreligious, interideological dialogue between Muslims and Hindus is to occur, then both the Muslim and the Hindu must come mainly to learn from each other; only then will it be "equal with equal," *par cum pari.* This rule also indicates that there can be no such thing as a one-way dialogue. For example,

Jewish-Christian discussions begun in the 1960's were mainly only prolegomena to interreligious dialogue. Understandably and properly, the Jews came to these exchanges only to teach Christians, although the Christians came mainly to learn. But, if authentic interreligious dialogue between Christians and Jews is to occur, then the Jews must also come mainly to learn; only will it then too be *par cum pari*.

EIGHTH COMMANDMENT: *Dialogue can take place only on the basis of mutual trust.* Although interreligious, interideological dialogue must occur with some kind of "corporate" dimension, that is, the participants must be involved as members of a religious or ideological community—for instance, as Marxists or Taoists—it is also fundamentally true that it is only *persons* who can enter into dialogue. But a dialogue among persons can be built only on personal trust. Hence it is wise not to tackle the most difficult problems in the beginning, but rather to approach first those issues most likely to provide some common ground, thereby establishing the basis of human trust. Then, gradually, as this personal trust deepens and expands, the more thorny matters can be undertaken. Thus, as in learning we move from the known to the unknown, so in dialogue we proceed from commonly held matters—which, given our mutual ignorance resulting from centuries of hostility, will take us quite some time to discover fully—to discuss matters of disagreement.

NINTH COMMANDMENT: *Persons entering into interreligious, interideological dialogue must be at least minimally self-critical of both themselves and their own religious or ideological traditions.* A lack of such self-criticism implies that one's own tradition already has all the correct answers. Such an attitude makes dialogue not only unnecessary, but even impossible, since we enter into dialogue primarily so *we* can learn—which obviously is impossible if our tradition has never made a misstep, if it has all the right answers. To be sure, in interreligious, interideological dialogue one must stand within a religious or ideological tradition with integrity and conviction, but such integrity and conviction must include, not exclude, a healthy self-criticism. Without it there can be no dialogue—and, indeed, no integrity.

TENTH COMMANDMENT: *Each participant eventually must attempt to experience the partner's religion or ideology "from within"*; for a religion or ideology is not merely something of the head, but also of the spirit, heart, and "whole being," individual and communal. John Dunne here speaks of "passing over" into another's religious or ideological experience and then coming back enlightened, broadened, and deepened. As Raimundo Panikkar notes, "To know what a religion says, we must understand what it says, but for this we must somehow believe in what it says": for example, "A Christian will never fully understand Hinduism if he is not, in one way or another, converted to Hinduism. Nor will a Hindu ever fully understand Christianity unless he, in one way or another, becomes Christian."

Interreligious, interideological dialogue operates in three areas: the practical, where we collaborate to help humanity; the depth or "spiritual" dimension where we attempt to experience the partner's religion or ideology "from within"; the cognitive, where we seek understanding and truth. Interreligious, interideological dialogue also has three phases. In the first phase we unlearn misinformation about each other and begin to know each other as we truly are. In phase two we begin to discern values in the partner's tradition and wish to appropriate them into our own tradition. For example, in the Buddhist-Christian dialogue Christians might learn a greater appreciation of the meditative tradition, and Buddhists might learn a greater appreciation of the prophetic, social justice tradition—both values traditionally strongly, though not exclusively, associated with the other's community. If we are serious, persistent, and sensitive enough in the dialogue, we may at times enter into phase three. Here we together begin to explore new areas of reality, of meaning, and of truth, of which neither of us had even been aware before. We are brought face to face with this new, as-yet-unknown-to-us dimension of reality only because of questions, insights, probings produced in the dialogue. We may thus dare to say that patiently pursued dialogue can become an instrument of new "re-velation," a further "unveiling" of reality—on which we must then act.

There is something radically different about phase one on the one hand and phases two and three on the other. In the latter we do not simply add on quantitatively another "truth" or value from the partner's tradition. Instead, as we assimilate it within our own religious self-understanding, it will proportionately transform our self-understanding. Since our dialogue partner will be in a similar position, we will then be able to witness authentically to those elements of deep value in our own tradition that our partner's tradition may well be able to assimilate with self-transforming profit. All this of course will have to be done with complete integrity on each side, each partner remaining authentically true to the vital core of his/her own religious tradition. However, in significant ways that vital core will be perceived and experienced differently under the influence of the dialogue, but, if the dialogue is carried on with both integrity and openness, the result will be that, for example, the Jew will be authentically Jewish and the Christian will be authentically Christian, not despite the fact that Judaism and/or Christianity have been profoundly "Buddhized," but because of it. And the same is true of a

Judaized and/or Christianized Buddhism. There can be no talk of a syncretism here, for syncretism means amalgamating various elements of different religions into some kind of a (con)fused whole without concern for the integrity of the religions involved—which is not the case with authentic dialogue.

Appendix 2
Review Questions
Dialogue Decalogue

NAME _____

Please answer these questions without reference to any specific religious tradition (your own or any other). Do not mention whether you are or are not religious or involved in a religious community.

1. Which of the directives in "The Dialogue Decalogue" would be the most difficult for you to put into practice if you participated in a dialogue with a person from a religious tradition other than your own (or any religious tradition, if you are not religious yourself)? *Give the number and a short explanation for your choice.*

2. Which of the directives in "The Dialogue Decalogue" would be the easiest for you to put into practice if you participated in a dialogue with a person from a religious tradition other than your own (or any religious tradition, if you are not religious yourself)? *Give the number and a short explanation for your choice.*

3. Although "The Dialogue Decalogue" is concerned with facilitating dialogue between persons, how would its general principles and ideals be helpful to studying religions in a way that did not involve dialogue with others (e.g., by reading textbooks, consulting online sources, reviewing professional articles and books, taking a college course, and so on)?

4. Optional topic-related question:

5. Optional topic- or course-related question:

Review Questions
Chapters 1 and 2

NAME _____

Please answer the following questions, citing the page(s) in the book where the answer if found.

1. The text offers a provisional description of religion, featuring four elements. What are the four elements?

    1. _____

    2. _____

    3. _____

    4. _____

2. Look up the word "intersubjective" in a collegiate dictionary, give its definition, and briefly explain how it relates to culture. (cite the dictionary you used for the definition)

3. Cite the three general approaches used to define religion and short description of each approach. Circle the number of the approach that you believe is the most helpful to understanding religion.

A. _____

B. _____

C. _____

4. Review pages 2 and 3 and in your own words, briefly explain what is meant by "sacred legitimation."

5. Aside from the "Provisional Description of Religion," which thinker's specific definition of religion presented in the text is the best? Name the thinker and give a short explanation for why his/her definition is the best.

6. A. Primal and Archaic religions are both classified as
   _____.

   B. What religious concept best reveals what is meant by the "anthropological" dimension of Axial Age religions.

7. Name three Axial Age visionaries and a transcendental religious concept (not a religion) associated with each.

Visionary	Concept
A.	
B.	
C.	

8. Research Question: Using two or more sources, research the census of the world's largest religions. What are the six largest religions in the world? Give the six in order of their size. Cite at least two sources you used in your research.

   1. _____

   2. _____

   3. _____

   4. _____

   5. _____

   6. _____

9. A. Transcendental religions affirm an Ultimate Power that is

_____, in contrast to pre-Axial religions that recog-

nized the Ultimate Power as (in various ways) related to

_____ or _____, itself. (same word in last two blanks)

   B. In what century did the transcendental worldview become a
   _____"large-scale cultural force in the West"?

10. Of the various books cited and analyzed in the text, list the three
    you would most like to read. List in order of your preference.

    A. _____

    B. _____

    C. _____

11. Aside from "intersubjective," give the definitions of three words
    you encountered in the reading that were not explicated in the
    text, and which you had to look up in a dictionary.

Brief Bibliography of Reliable Texts in Religious Studies

In addition to the texts noted here, readers are encouraged to review bibliographies found in general textbooks. A number of the texts noted here can be found in earlier (or later) editions than those cited, so look for authors and titles as cited and use later editions if available. As a rule, later editions are better than earlier editions.

Reference and General Texts

Encyclopedias and Dictionaries (General)

Bowker, John, ed. *The Concise Oxford Dictionary of World Religions.* Oxford: Oxford University Press, 2000.

Hinnells, John R., ed. *Dictionary of Religions: From Abraham to Zoroaster.* Harmondsworth, England: Penguin, 1986.

Jones, Lindsay, ed. *The Encyclopedia of Religion.* 2nd ed. 15 vols. Farmington Hills, MI: Macmillan/Thomson Gale, 2005.

Levinson, David. *Religion: A Cross-Cultural Encyclopedia.* 1 vol. New York: Oxford University Press, 1998.

Melton, J. Gordon, and Martin Baumann, eds. *Religions of the World: A Comprehensive Encyclopedia of Beliefs and Practices.* 2nd ed. 6 vols. Santa Barbara, CA: ABC-CLIO, 2010.

General Texts (Religious Studies)

Capps, Walter H. *Religious Studies: The Making of a Discipline.* Minneapolis: Fortress Press, 1995.

Durkheim, Elile. *Elementary Forms of Religious Life.* New York: Free Press, 1965.

Eliade, Mircea. *The Sacred and the Profane.* New York: Harper Torchbooks, 1961.

_____, and Joseph M. Kitagawa. *The History of Religions: Essays in Methodology.* Chicago: University of Chicago Press, 1959.

Lessa, William A., and Evon Z. Vogt. *Reader in Comparative Religion: An Anthropological Approach.* New York: Harper & Row, 1965.

Pals, Daniel L. *Eight Theories of Religion.* 2nd ed. New York: Oxford University Press, 2006.

Stone, Jon R., ed. *The Craft of Religions Studies.* New York: St. Martin's Press, 1998.

Taylor, Mark C., ed. *Critical Terms for Religious Studies.* Chicago: University of Chicago Press, 1998.

Waardenburg, Jacques. *Classical Approaches to the Study of Religion.* New York: Walter de Gruyter, 1999.

Wach, Joachim. *The Comparative Study of Religion.* New York: Columbia Univ. Press, 1958.

General Texts (World Religions)

Carmody, Denise L., and John Carmody. *The Story of The World Religions.* Mountain View, CA: Mayfield, 1988.

Corrigan, John, et al. *Jews, Christians, Muslims: A Comparative Introduction to Monotheistic Religions.* Upper Saddle River: NJ: Prentice Hall, 1998.

Ellwood, Robert S., and Barbara A. McGraw. *Many Peoples, Many Faiths.* 10th ed. Upper Saddle River, NJ: Prentice Hall, 2014.

Esposito, John L., Darrell J. Fasching, and Todd Lewis. *World Religions Today.* 3rd ed. New York: Oxford University Press, 2009.

Fasching, Darrell, and Dell deChant. *Comparative Religious Ethics: A Narrative Approach.* Oxford, UK: Blackwell, 2001.

Hutchinson, John A. *Paths of Faith.* 4th ed. New York: McGraw-Hill, 1991.

Matthews, Warren. *World Religions.* 7th ed. Belmont, CA: Wadsworth, 2012.

Neusner, Jacob, ed. *World Religions in America.* 4th ed. Louisville: Westminster John Knox, 2009.

Nigosian, S. A. *World Religions: A Historical Approach.* 3rd. ed. Boston: Bedford/St. Martin's, 2000.

Smart, Ninian. *The World's Religions.* 2nd. ed. Cambridge, UK: Cambridge University Press, 1998.

_____ , and Richard D. Hecht, eds. *Sacred Texts of the World: A Universal Anthology.* New York: Crossroad, 1982.

Smith, Huston. *The World's Religions.* New York: Harper San Francisco, 1992.

VanVoorst, Robert E., ed. *Anthology of World Scriptures.* 7th ed. Independence, KY: Cengage Learning, 2011.

Wilson, Andrew, ed. *World Scripture: A Comparative Anthology of Sacred Texts.* New York: Paragon House, 1991.

Young, William A. *The World's Religions: World Views and Contemporary Issues.* Englewood Cliffs, NJ: Prentice Hall, 1995.

Selected Texts on Religious Traditions

Buddhism

Conze, Edward. *Buddhism: Its Essence and Development.* New York: Harper Torchbooks, 1959.

Harvey, Peter. *An Introduction to Buddhism: Teachings, History, Practices.* Cambridge, UK: Cambridge University Press, 1990.

LeFleur, William. *Buddhism: A Cultural Perspective.* Upper Saddle River, NJ: Prentice Hall, 1988.

Rahula, Walpola. *What the Buddha Taught.* New York: Evergreen Press, 1962.

Robinson, Richard H., and Willard L. Johnson. *The Buddhist Religion.* Belmont, CA: Wadsworth, 1982.

Christianity

Carmody, Denise Lardner. *Jesus: An Introduction.* Belmont, CA: Wadsworth, 1987.

Manschreck, Clyde. *A History of Christianity in the World.* 2nd ed. Upper Saddle, NJ: Prentice Hall, 1974.

Niebuhr, H. Richard. *Christ and Culture.* New York: Harper & Row, 1951.

Tillich, Paul. *A History of Christian Thought.* New York: Harper & Row, 1968.

Walker, Wiliston. *A History of the Christian Church.* rev. ed. New York: Scribners, 1984.

East Asian Religions (Confucianism and Daoism)

Creel, H. G. *Confucius and the Chinese Way.* New York: Harper Torchbooks, 1960.

Jochim, Christian. *Chinese Religion: A Cultural Perspective.* Englewood Cliffs, NJ: Prentice Hall, 1986.

Lopez, Donald S., ed. *Religions of China in Practice.* Princeton, NJ: Princeton University Press, 1996.

Thompson, Laurence G. *Chinese Religion.* Belmont, CA: Wadsworth, 1989.

Welch, Holmes. *Taoism: The Parting of the Way.* Boston: Beacon Press, 1957.

Hinduism

Brockington, J. L. *The Sacred Thread: Hinduism in Its Continuity and Diversity.* New York: Columbia University Press, 1981.

Herman, A. L. *Brief Introduction to Hinduism: Religion, Philosophy, and Ways of Liberation.* Boulder, CO: Westview Press, 1991.

Hopkins, Thomas. *The Hindu Religious Tradition.* Belmont, CA: Wadsworth, 1982.

Kinsley, David R. *Hinduism: A Cultural Perspective.* Englewood Cliffs, NJ: Prentice Hall, 1982.

Klostermaier, Klaus K. *A Survey of Hinduism.* Albany: State University Press, 1989.

Islam

Asad, Muhammad. *The Message of the Quran.* Gibralter: Dar al-Andalus, 1980.

Esposito, John. *Islam: The Straight Path.* Oxford (updated with new epilogue), UK: Oxford University Press, 2005.

Haneef, Suzanne. *What Everyone Should Know About Islam and Muslims.* Chicago: Kazi Publications, 1996.

Peters, F. E. *Muhammad and the Origins of Islam.* Albany: State University Press, 1994.

Rahman, Fazlur. *Major Themes of the Quran.* 2nd ed. Bibliotheca Islamica, 1989.

Judaism

Bamberger, Bernard J. *The Story of Judaism.* New York: Schochen Books, 1970.

Fackenheim, Emil. *What Is Judaism?* New York: Summit Books, 1987.

Johnson, Paul. *A History of the Jews.* New York: Harper & Row, 1987.

Neusner, Jacob. *Self-fulfilling Prophecy: Exile and Return in the History of Judaism.* Boston: Beacon Press, 1987.

_____ . *The Way of the Torah: An Introduction to Judaism.* 2nd ed. Encino, CA: Dickenson, 1974.

New Religious Movements

Bednorowski, Mary F. *New Religions and the Theological Imagination in America.* Bloomington: Indiana University Press, 1989.

Ellwood, Robert S., and Harry B. Partin. *Religious and Spiritual Groups in Modern America.* 2nd ed. Englewood Cliffs, NJ: Prentice Hall, 1988.

Hunt, Stephen J. *Alternative Religions: A Sociological Introduction.* Burlington, VT: Ashgate, 2003.

Miller, Timothy, ed. *America's Alternative Religions.* Albany: State University Press, 1995.

Melton, J. Gordon. *Encyclopedia Handbook of Cults in America.* rev. ed. New York: Garland, 1992.

Moore, Laurence. *Religious Outsiders and the Making of America.* New York: Oxford University Press, 1987.

Selected Texts on Miscellaneous Topics

America (the U.S.A.) and Religion(s)

Albanese, Catherine L. *America: Religions and Religion.* 5th ed. Independence, KY: Cengage Learning, 2012.

Eck, Diana L. *A New Religious America.* San Francisco: Harper San Francisco, 2001.

Finke, Roger, and Rodney Stark. *The Churching of America, 1776–1990: Winners and Losers in Our Religious Economy.* New Brunswick, NJ: Rutgers University Press, 2000.

Gaustad, Edwin Scott. *A Religious History of America.* New York: Harper & Row, 1966.

Hudson, Winthrop S. *Religion in America.* New York: Scribners, 1965.

Economics and Religion(s)

Giddens, Anthony. *Capitalism and Modern Social Theory: An Analysis of the Writings of Marx, Durkheim, and Max Weber.* Cambridge: Cambridge University Press, 1971.

Green, Robert W., (ed.). *Protestantism and Capitalism: The Weber Thesis and Its Critics.* Boston: D.C. Heath & Co., 1959.

Miller, Vincent J. *Consuming Religion: Christian Faith and Practice In A Consumer Culture.* New York: Continuum, 2004.

Weber, Max. *The Protestant Ethic and the Spirit of Capitalism.* Translated by Talcott Parsons. New York: Charles Scribner's Sons, 1958.

Ethics and Religion(s)

Carmody, Denise Lardner, and John Tully Carmody. *How to Live Well: Ethics in the World Religions.* Belmont, CA: Wadsworth, 1988.

Crawford, S. Cromwell. *World Religions and Global Ethics.* New York: Paragon House, 1989.

Fasching, Darrell, and Dell deChant. *Comparative Religious Ethics: A Narrative Approach.* Oxford, UK: Blackwell, 2001.

Little, David, and Sumner B. Twiss. *Comparative Religious Ethics: A New Method*. San Francisco: Harper & Row, 1978.

Stackhouse, Max L. *Creeds, Society, and Human Rights*. Grand Rapids, MI: Eerdmans, 1984.

Nature (the Environment) and Religion(s)

Bauman, Whitney A., Bohannon, Richard R., II, and O'Brien, Kevin J., eds. *Grounding Religion: A Field Guide to the Study of Religion and Ecology*. New York: Routledge, 2011.

Gottlieb, Roger S., ed. *Oxford Handbook of Religion and Ecology*. New York: Oxford University Press, 2008.

Taylor, Bron, *Dark Green Religion*. Berkeley, CA: University of California Press, 2010.

_____, ed. *Encyclopedia of Religion and Nature*. London: Continuum, 2008.

White, Lynn, Jr. "The Historical Roots of Our Ecological Crisis," in *Science* 155 (1967) 1203–1207. (Also in *Science*, 1974: 15–31).

Popular Culture and Religion(s)

Chidester, David. *Authentic Fakes: Religion and American Popular Culture* (Berkeley, CA: University of California Press, 2005.

Clark, Terry Ray and Dan W. Clanton, Jr., eds. *Understanding Religion and Popular Culture*. London: Routledge, 2012.

deChant, Dell. *The Sacred Santa: Religious Dimensions of Consumer Culture*. Cleveland: The Pilgrim Press, 2002.

Forbes, Bruce David, and Jeffrey H. Mahan, eds. *Religion and Popular Culture in America*. 2nd ed. Berkeley: University of California Press, 2005.

Mazur, Eric Michael, and Kate McCarthy. *God in the Details: American Religion in Popular Culture*. New York: Routledge, 2001.

Secularization and Religion(s)

Berger, Peter. *The Sacred Canopy*. Garden City, NY: Doubleday/Anchor, 1969.

Bruce, Steve. *Religion in the Modern World: From Cathedrals to Cults*. Oxford, UK: Oxford University Press, 1996.

_____ . *God Is Dead: Secularization in the West*. Oxford, UK: Blackwell, 2002.

Chadwick, Owen. *The Secularization of the European Mind in the Nineteenth Century*. Cambridge, UK: Cambridge University Press, 1975.

Martin, David. *On Secularization: Towards a Revised General Theory*. Burlington, VT: Ashgate, 2005.

Pecora, Vincent P. *Secularization and Cultural Criticism*. Chicago: University of Chicago Press, 2006.

Swatos, William H., Jr., and Daniel V. A. Olson, ed. *The Secularization Debate*. Lanham, MD: Rowman and Littlefield, 2000.

Sports and Religion(s)

Hoffman, Shirl J., ed. *Sport and Religion*. Champaign, IL: Human Kinetics Books, 1992.

Prebish, Charles S. *Religion and Sport: The Meeting of the Sacred and the Profane*. Westport, CT: Greenwood Press, 1993.

Price, Joseph L., ed. *From Season to Season: Sports as American Religion*. Macon, GA: Mercer University Press, 2001.

_____ . *Rounding the Bases: Baseball and Religion in America*. Macon, GA: Mercer University Press, 2006.

Williams, Peter. *The Sports Immortals: Deifying the American Athlete*. Bowling Green, OH: Bowling Green State University Popular Press, 1994.

Women in Religion(s)

Carmody, Denise Lardner. *Women and World Religions.* Englewood Cliffs, NJ: Prentice Hall, 1989.

Gross, Rita M., ed. *Beyond Androcentrism: New Essay on Women and Religion.* Missoula, MT: Scholars Press, 1977.

Haddad, Yvonne Yazback, and Ellison Banks Findly, ed. *Women, Religion and Social Change.* Albany: State University Press, 1985.

Sharma, Arvind, ed. *Today's Woman in World Religions.* Albany: State University Press, 1994.

Wessinger, Catherine, ed. *Women's Leadership in Marginal Religions.* Urbana, IL: University of Illinois Press, 1993.

Index

history, classification of religion and, 12, 13–14
human products, culture and, 3–4
"humps and lumps," 77, 78

Idea of the Holy, The (Otto), 6–7
incarnation, 14
Industrial Revolution
 inventions of, 51–52
 Marx on, 52–53
Interstate Highway Act, 67
Iraq war, 74
Islam
 "disenchantment" concept and, 34
 inception of, 30
 as transcendental, 16
Islamic State in Iraq and the Levant (ISIL), 74, 84

Jainism
 Axial Age and, 22–23
 religion and culture, 13
Jameson, Fredric, 68–69
Jaspers, Karl, 22
jiva, 23
Judaism
 Axial Age and, 23–24, 25
 "disenchantment" concept and, 34, 46
 Roman Empire and, 43
 as transcendental, 16

Kay, John, 51
Kellner, Douglas, 68–69
"kill-for-ism," 64, 75
King, Martin Luther, Jr., 67, 76

Lakeland, Paul, 65
Lambert, Yves, 59
Lao Tze, 23
legitimation, 3, 69–70
li, 23
Luther, Martin, 46–47

"magical thought," 69
Mahavira, 22–23
mana, 15, 27
Martin, David, 59–60
Marx, Karl, 5–6, 52–53
medieval period, Dark Ages and, 50
megachurches, 78, 79
meta-myths, 10, 29–30, 32
modernity
 postmodernity and, 66–69, 75, 76–77
 religion in contemporary culture and, 62–66
 religious resurgence and secularization thesis, 78
monotheism
 Axial Age and, 32–35
 defined, 14–15
 Judaism and, 23–24
Moore, Sally F., 11
Myerhoff, Barbara G., 11
mysterium tremendum et fascinans, 82
"mythico-ritual" dynamism, 12
myths
 defined, 10–12
 religious resurgence and, 83

nature, as sacred, 32, 82–83
"neo-cosmological" approach, to religious resurgence, 80, 81–83
Nicea, Council of, 43
Niebuhr, H. Richard, 1
Nietzsche, Friedrich, 54, 76
nirvana, 23

Origin and Goal of History, The (Jaspers), 22
Otto, Rudolf, 6–7, 8, 82

Pals, Daniel L., 4
Passion of the Christ, The (film), 78, 79
Peace of Westphalia, 48
Pecora, Vincent, 59
Persia, Zoroastrianism and, 23
philosophic tradition

Printed in the USA
CPSIA information can be obtained
at www.ICGtesting.com
JSHW012021270724
67088JS00002B/25